characters (principal person)

Themes / Motifs / Style (what theme stood out to you)

summary of book (main points)

key ideas / arguments (intresting ideas)

South of Main

your evaluation (key points)

Landmarks of the Southside

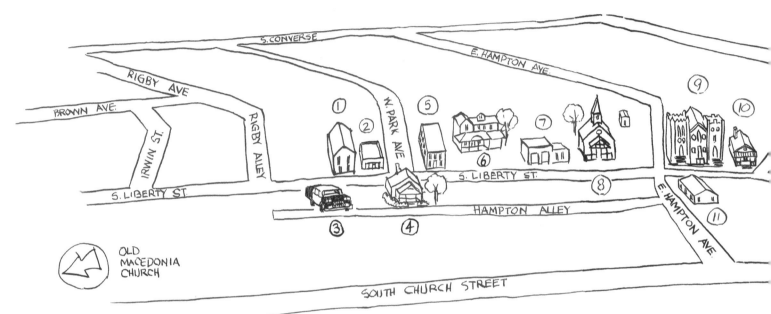

OLD MACEDONIA CHURCH

1. BULL'S CLINIC
2. OLIVER'S PHARMACY
3. DELUXE CAB
4. THE HOME OF MARY H. WRIGHT
5. COLLINS HOTEL
6. COLLINS FUNERAL HOME
7. COLLINS SERVICE STATION
8. EPIPHANY CHURCH & KINDERGARTEN
9. MAJORITY BAPTIST CHURCH
10. THE YOUNG/WOODSON HOME

11. THE BLUE LANTERN
12. SOUTHSIDE CAFE
13. BYRD STREET KINDERGARTEN
14. FREEMAN'S CEMETERY
15. DAWKINS SMITH FUNERAL
16. MOUNT MORIAH BAPTIST CHURCH
17. CARVER HIGH SCHOOL
18. TOBE HARTWELL APARTMENTS
19. CARRIER STREET SCHOOL
20. THE USO
21. MARY H. WRIGHT ELEMENTARY SCHOOL

NOTE: THERE WERE MORE THAN 900 HOMES
AND BUSINESSES IN THIS NEIGHBORHOOD IN 1970.
THESE ARE SOME OF THE MAJOR LANDMARKS.

South of Main

compiled by

Beatrice Hill
Brenda Lee

photo portraits by

Raymond Floyd

HUB CITY
writers project

Spartanburg ◇ 2005

Second printing, March 2005

Hub City editors: Betsy Wakefield Teter, Melissa Walker and Linda Powers
Proofreaders: Carol Bradof, Tom Johnson, Jill McBurney
Editorial assistant: Pamela Ivey
Title page graphic: Scott Cunningham
Mapping researcher: Abigail Seitz
Cover and book design: Mark Olencki
Author photographs: Mark Olencki
Scanning: Katherine Wakefield, Mark Olencki and Christina Smith
Printed by McNaughton & Gunn, Inc., Saline, MI

Hub City Writers Project
Post Office Box 8421
Spartanburg, South Carolina 29305
(864) 577-9349 • fax (864) 577-0188 • www.hubcity.org

ISBN, 1-891885-45-6, soft cover
ISBN, 1-891885-46-4, hard cover

Publication of this book is funded in part by the Arts Partnership of Greater Spartanburg and its donors, the County and City of Spartanburg, and the South Carolina Arts Commission which receives funding from the National Endowment for the Arts and the John and Susan Bennett Memorial Arts Fund of the Coastal Community Foundation of South Carolina.

"No historical areas are involved in the project activities."

—a line from the federal urban renewal grant application
by the City of Spartanburg in October 1970

"It was an American tragedy."

—James Cheek

The Hub City Writers Project thanks its friends who made contributions in support of this book:

**The Arts Partnership of Greater Spartanburg
The Phifer/Johnson Foundation
The South Carolina Arts Commission
The South Carolina Humanities Council
The Spartanburg County Public Libraries**

Greg & Lisa Atkins
Paula & Stan Baker
Isabel & John Barber
Valerie & Bill Barnet
Barnet LLC
Carol & Jim Bradof

Bea & Dennis Bruce
Harrison Chapman
Cleveland/White Realtors
Colonial Trust Company
The Rev. & Mrs. David A. Fort
Donald L. Fowler

Stewart & Ann Johnson
Dr. & Mrs. Julian Josey
Sara, Paul & Ellis Lehner
Dr. & Mrs. Thomas McDaniel
Dwight & Liz Patterson
Bette Wakefield

John & Ruth Abercrombie
Richard T. Adams
Margaret Allen
Dr. & Mrs. Mitchell H. Allen
C. Mack Amick
Callis J. Anderson Jr.
Arkwright Foundation
Atchison Transportation Services
Tom & Ceci Arthur
Dr. & Mrs. James Bearden III
Charles & Christi Bebko
Shirley Blaes
Walter & Mabel Brice
Susan Bridges
Ann Brown
William & Katherine Burns
Dr. Alma Wand & Wallace Byrd
Katherine & Marvin Cann
Ruth L. Cate
Mr. & Mrs. M.L. Cates Jr.
Mr. & Mrs. John Chapman
Liz Chapman
Mr. & Mrs. Robert H. Chapman III
Mr. & Mrs. James T. Clamp, Jr.
Robert & Janeen Cochran
Sally & Jerry Cogan Jr.

Mr. & Mrs. Richard Conn
Mr. & Mrs. Richard L. Conner
Matthew Corbin
Helen & Ben Correll
Paul & Nancy Coté
Tom Moore Craig
John & Kirsten Cribb
Wilhelmina S. Dearybury
Fredrick B. Dent
Georgie & Bill Dickerson
Isaac Dickson
Chris & Alice Dorrance
Jimmy & Becky Dunbar
Susan Willis & James Dunlap
Dr. & Mrs. William C. Elston
Ginger & Bob Elwell
Edwin Epps
Jacqueline Douglas Farr
John & Nora Beth Featherston
Dr. & Mrs. George Fields Jr.
Elsie Finkelstein
First South Bank
Russel & Susan Floyd
Anne & Larry Flynn
Keller Cushing Freeman
Dr. & Mrs. J. Sidney Fulmer

Mr. & Mrs. William P. Gee
Marsha & Jimmy Gibbs
Ralph Gillespie
Girl Scouts of the Piedmont
  Area Council
Ellen Goldey
Margaret & Chip Green
Lucy Grier
Mr. & Mrs. Tom Grier
Susan Griswold & John Morton
Jim & Kay Gross
Marianna & Roger Habisreutinger
Lee & Kitty Hagglund
Benjamin & Tanya Hamm
Jerry L. Hardee
Emma D. Harrington
Peyton & Michele Harvey
Calvin & Ann Lee Hastie, *in
  memory of Costella Coln Foster*
Eaddy Williams Hayes
Judy & Keith Haynes
Donald & Alice Hatcher Henderson
Gary & Carmela Henderson
Mike & Nancy Henderson
Beatrice Hill
Charlie Hodge

Mr. & Mrs. Tom Hollis
Marion Peter Holt, *in memory of Queenie E. Boyd*
Eugenia Hooker
Doug & Marilyn Hubbell
Mr. & Mrs. Kenneth R. Huckaby
James Hudgens
Debra Hutchins
David & Harriet Ike
Mrs. James Ivy
Inman Riverdale Foundation
Sadie Jackson
Dr. & Mrs. Vernon Jeffords
Thomas L. Johnson
Wallace Johnson
Mr. & Mrs. Charles W. Jones
Lewis & Denny Jones
Frannie Jordan
Peggy & Greg Karpick
Peggy & Charles D. Kay
Ann J. Kelly & Don Haughay
Mr. & Mrs. Thomas B. Ketchum
Jerry King
Bert & Ruth Knight
Klaus Kolb
Mary Jane & Cecil Lanford
Mr. and Mrs. Jack W. Lawrence
Law Insurance Agency
Wood & Janice Lay
Brenda Lee, in memory of Stella
Ezell Coln
Joe & Ruth Lesesne
George & Frances Loudon
Brownlee & Julie Lowry
Mary Speed & Manning Lynch
Robert & Nancy Lyon
Michael Lythgoe
Anthony & Jeraldine Mack and daughters, Simone & Monica
Don Martin State Farm Insurance Companies
Zerno E. Martin Jr.
Gaines H. Mason
Dan & Kit Maultsby

Jill & John McBurney
Gail & Bob McCullough
Pat M. McDonald
Mr. & Mrs. Larry McGehee
Fayssoux McLean
Ed & Gail Medlin
Mr. & Mrs. Lewis Miller
Karen & Bob Mitchell
Nancy & Lawrence Moore
George D. Mullinax
Mr. & Mrs. Douglas B. Nash
National Bank of South Carolina
Virginia New
Vivian Fisher & Jim Newcome
Alexander Nichols
Margaret & George Nixon
Corry & Amy Oakes
Olencki Graphics, Inc.
PRM Consulting, Inc.
Frazer Pajak
Steve Parker
Mr. & Mrs. W. Keith Parris
Waddell "Wally P" Pearson
Richard Pennell
Mr. & Mrs. Edward P. Perrin
Craig & Kay Phillips
Mickey & Nancy Pierce
Mr. & Mrs. Robert V. Pinson
Andrew Poliakoff
John & Lynne Poole
Robert D. Porter
Mrs. Roy S. Powell
Norman Powers
Elizabeth & W.O. Pressley Jr.
Harry Price
Phil & Frances Racine
Eileen N. Rampey
Mr. & Mrs. William B. Ramsey III
Karen Randall
Allison & John Ratterree
Glenn Reese
James L. & Betty E. Reynolds
Nancy & Robert Riehle
Harold Risher

Elisabeth Robe
Martial & Amy Robichaud
Harold & Ollie Robinson
Richard Rumley & family
Steve & Elena Rush
Muffet & Olin Sansbury
Carol & Mark Scott
John & Sue Scott
Doug Smith
Mr. & Mrs. B.G. Stephens
Eliot & Michel Stone
Mr. & Mrs. George Stone
James "Patch" Talley, *in memory of Vicey Rice*
Nancy Taylor
Billy C. Terry
Betsy Teter & John Lane
Delphine Osburn Thornton
Bob and Cheryl Tillotson
Tire Corral Inc.
Dewey & Kitty Tullis, *in memory of Ernest Collins*
Sarah van Rens
Unique Services of the Upstate Inc.
Urban League of the Upstate
Mr. & Mrs. Jay Wakefield
Melissa Walker & Chuck Reback
John Wardlaw
Costella Watson & Edward Miller
Billy & Lindsay Webster
David & Kathy Weir
Peter & Kathie Weisman
Sara & Richard Wheeler
Dave & Linda Whisnant
Mr. and Mrs, John B. White, Jr.
Edith Whitmire
Leon Wiles
Brenda Wingo
Dennis & Annemarie Wiseman
Mr. & Mrs. Emerson Fort Wolfe Jr.
Doris Wright, *in memory of Ted Wright*
Susan Young
Kurt & Nell Zimmerli

Table of Contents

Introduction

~Carmen Harris~

The African-American community presented in *South of Main* exists only in the historical memory of the people who lived there. Were it not for this book, the memory of the community might completely vanish. Scholars of African-American history recognize the tendency to devalue an already fragile African-American past. The matter became personal for me when my family visited the cemetery at Mount Vernon, the home of George Washington. The Washington family graves could only be observed from a respectful distance. We knew who they were because of detailed grave headstones. George and Martha's coffins were the most remote—sitting encased in marble slabs in a mausoleum. In the slave cemetery, there were no headstones. There was a concrete slab placed at the site by the Ladies of Mount Vernon Society in 1929. It included the words "faith, hope, love," words from the Bible (I Corinthians 13:13), imposed upon these long-dead slaves by the Ladies who selected the inscription. There also is a newer memorial—a circular bench—designed by architecture students from Howard University in 1983 that includes the same three words. People were having their pictures taken sitting atop the bones of dead slaves. I was deeply troubled by the unspoken message: even in death, these blacks whose labor made the Washington family wealth did not deserve equal reverence.

On a grander scale, lack of respect for African Americans, and the institutions they built, has led to insensitivity to the value of black communities. Politicians and financiers have shown a willingness to erase such communities, regardless of their histories, in the name of "progress." Since the 1960s, many African-American communities have been dismembered by urban renewal, a program that promised to modernize racially-segregated neighborhoods but which, in most cases, obliterated them. The end of the Spartanburg's roughly century-old Southside community is a particular case in point.

The introductory chapter of this book, "Evolution of a Neighborhood," documents the life of Joseph Miles Young, one of the early citizens of the Southside, and his wife, Priscilla Young, who came to the area about the time of the Civil War. During Reconstruction they and other former slaves began to acquire land and to build lives. Young and his neighbors defy the general stereotype of ex-slaves being hapless and unable to provide for themselves. That blacks built this community from the ground up demonstrates that African Americans fully understood the opportunities that freedom held and intended to seize them.

The history of the Southside's development shows that while whites were concerned about "reconstructing" what they had, African Americans worked to build communities and a people from the ground up for themselves and for their children. They built churches where they could worship according to their understanding of Christianity rather than to continue to attend white churches where ministers had preached to them that the Bible directed slaves to obey their masters. Some Spartanburg whites refused to pay local taxes to support the state's first-ever free public school system—not because they rejected public education but because they opposed educating ex-slaves. Therefore, founders of the Southside used their churches as schools, and when they could afford it, they built schools for their children who became teachers, ministers, health workers, and businesspeople in the community. The Southside grew, but it was unable to provide the public works that are essential to sustaining a community. By the late 1950s the eighty-year-old community entered a state of decline from which it never recovered. Most of it was demolished during the 1970s and, in some cases, white Spartanburg has inched slowly into its place.

During its existence, the Southside served as a cornerstone of Afro-Spartan life. Former residents' recollections reconstruct a supportive and nurturing community. While many of the Southside's leading residents were descendants of Joseph and Priscilla Young, neighbors also shared a fictive kinship in which familial concern extended beyond blood relatives. Cora Byrd Taylor and Wilhelmina Hollis recalled that the adults in the neighborhood considered all children their responsibility. "If your parents had to work, the neighbors watched you," Hollis remembered. Her recollections reflect the African proverb "It takes a village to raise a child." Community parenting had been an important survival skill of enslaved African Americans and one that continued in communities where African-American women's work remained vital to family survival.

The Southside was a center of black entrepreneurship. Willie Wilson recalled making deliveries for the local grocer. There were doctors, barbers, dry cleaners, an ice cream parlor, eating establishments, cab companies, funeral parlors, and even a mini-golf course. Retired U.S. Judge Matthew J. Perry, who played a prominent role in the civil rights movement in South Carolina, had an office in the Southside at one time. There were pockets of vice as well. According to Wilson, respectable members of the Southside frowned upon the activities that occurred in these places. As the Southside experienced increased levels of absentee ownership, many structures fell into disrepair.

The chapter here entitled "The Southside in Urban Renewal" illustrates how the convergence of the civil rights revolution and the war on poverty— both intended to assimilate African Americans into American society—became a double-edged sword. African Americans expected that legal equality and economic opportunity would lead to the incorporation of their communities and institutions into the mainstream. Southside residents never imagined that the neighborhood in which generations proudly had invested money, sweat, and blood to create, and which they valued so deeply, was too dilapidated to save. Fannie Richie expected that a revitalized Southside would remain a complete community. Former Spartanburg Mayor James Talley thought the plan would remove only substandard housing and replace it. That didn't happen. Investments in businesses and in nice homes did not immunize them from destruction to make way for "progress." In the aftermath many former residents recognized what had been lost.

The probable outcome of the "revitalization" plan was not unforeseen. The late John C. West, who was Lieutenant Governor in 1969, observed that residents' personal feelings had not been considered in such projects. As this book points out, demolition occurred simultaneously with desegregation, and the symbolic violence with which parts of the community was razed could be perceived as punitive. More insulting to former residents' feelings was that as late as a decade later, areas where blacks once built lives remained empty. West's recognition that a sense of place is central to identity was an astute observation. Coherent neighborhoods like the Southside created middle-class morals and ethics that had a positive effect on residents. When 2,000 Southside residents were dispersed to other areas, that moral compass was dismantled. The middle-class models of achievement went one way. Their poorer neighbors went another: many entered public housing (if they could get in) where hopelessness and worse became their morals and ethics.

According to this book, more than 1,400 communities across the United States, the majority of them African-American, faced the same fate as the Southside. In my hometown of Gaffney, twenty miles east, the corner where my uncle's gas station stood, as well as the dilapidated Carnegie Library for blacks behind it, is now an asphalt parking lot. But there is much to preserve and to revere—even if it can only be done in books like this one. The narratives of the rise and demise of the Southside neighborhood bring my mind again to Mount Vernon, to the slave cemetery, to the missing markers, to the anonymity of black people whose contributions enriched a community. The residents of the Southside were similarly anonymous. The demolition of the community and the paving over of its memories has imposed a view that the Southside is not a place worth remembering. Beatrice Hill and Brenda Lee, compilers of much of this history, and the other writers of the Hub City Writers Project are to be commended for "marking the grave" of the Southside, for giving voice to the "faith, hope, and love" of a black community that was born in the 1860s during the first Reconstruction and died during the second Reconstruction of the 1960s.

⬦ Carmen V. Harris is a Gaffney native and resides in Simpsonville with her husband and daughters. She earned two degrees from Clemson, has a doctorate in history from Michigan State University and teaches history at USC Upstate.

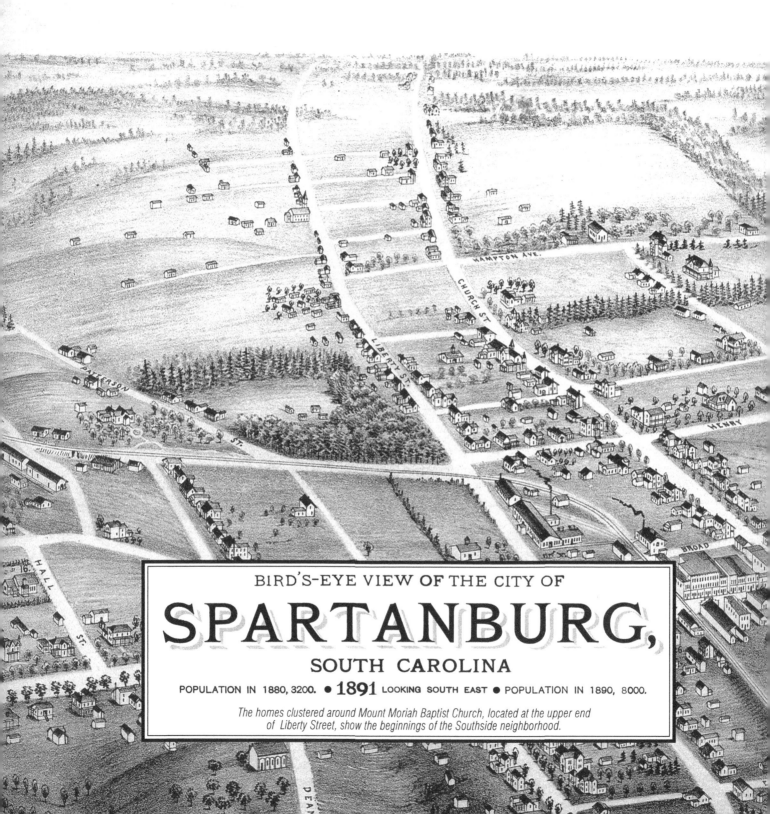

BIRD'S-EYE VIEW OF THE CITY OF

SPARTANBURG,

SOUTH CAROLINA

POPULATION IN 1880, 3200. • **1891** LOOKING SOUTH EAST • POPULATION IN 1890, 8000.

*The homes clustered around Mount Moriah Baptist Church, located at the upper end
of Liberty Street, show the beginnings of the Southside neighborhood.*

1

Evolution
of a Neighborhood

A FEW YEARS AFTER THE END OF THE CIVIL WAR, a short walk south of Spartanburg's Main Street, a small group of African Americans and their families lived together at the end of a dusty road called Liberty Street. Recently emancipated, they gathered as a new community during a dangerous time when the violent activity of the Ku Klux Klan was at its peak across the South Carolina Piedmont. The 1870 census tells us they were farmers, blacksmiths, and tradesmen, and family names included Clemmons, Young, and Gray, among others. By 1880 the small group had grown to 17 men and their families and included three carpenters, a barber, and a minister named Julius Steele.

There were no paved roads or streetlights in Spartanburg at that time. At the end of the Civil War almost everyone in town lived north of Main Street, on the fringes of Wofford College. Nearly all of the newly-freed black families lived in areas behind the large antebellum homes on both sides of North Church Street. Whites outnumbered blacks in Spartanburg, but just barely; the city's 1868 voter registration roll lists 406 white male voters and 254 black male voters. The city was just beginning to grow south then, and over the next decade wealthy white families would begin constructing their Victorian mansions

Professor C.C. Woodson, principal of Carver High, in the early 1940s. He is standing on the steps of Mount Moriah Church. ~Courtesy, Patricia Nichols

along both sides of South Church Street, getting closer to the tiny enclave of black families who founded the Southside neighborhood.

The most prominent of those black Southside pioneers was an **enterprising man named Joseph Miles Young**, a 52-year-old mattress-maker and upholsterer, who lived at the end of Liberty Street in 1870 with his wife, Priscilla, a 38-year-old homemaker, and eight children ranging in age from one to 20. Over the next three decades several of his children and their spouses would go on to **distinguish themselves in the fields of education and business**; one of their grandchildren, C.C. Woodson Jr., would serve as principal of Carver High for 30 years.

The circumstances of Joseph Young's arrival in Spartanburg are not recorded on any official documents. **Yet his second son curiously bore the same name as the notorious Sea Island slave owner Pierce Butler**, which **indicates the family might have come to Spartanburg from the Georgia coast**. In 1859 plantation owner Pierce M. Butler held the largest single sale of human beings in United States history in Savannah, Georgia, when he auctioned off 428 slaves, half his holdings, in an effort to raise cash. **The 1870 census indicates Joseph and Priscilla Young came to South Carolina from Georgia** sometime in 1859 or 1860; their son Kenneth was born in Georgia in 1859 while their daughter Louisa was born in South Carolina the next year. Known records are inadequate to link Spartanburg's Joseph M. Young, who was born in North Carolina, to Pierce Butler or to the 1859 slave sale, but the name of Young's second child, Pierce Butler Young, and the family's arrival from Georgia by 1860 suggest a connection between the two.

Wherever his origins, Joseph **Young quickly established himself as one of the most industrious men in Spartanburg's growing African-American community**. At the time of the 1870 census, he already owned real estate valued at $400 and personal property valued at $200, significant holdings for a black or white person at the time. There are **no records** to indicate how Young acquired this property, but in the **years** after the Civil War, a skilled mattress-maker/

upholsterer could have prospered in a growing industrial town like Spartanburg by serving the needs of the city's growing upper middle class. Young may have been able to save the money for land purchases from his earnings. He may also have worked for prominent whites who befriended him and sold him land at a fair price. Or he could have brought assets with him: Young is listed in the 1870 census as "mulatto," meaning one of his parents or grandparents likely was white, potentially giving him a favored status with a slave-owning family.

Between 1873 and 1900 Joseph and Priscilla diligently added to their land-holdings on the Southside, buying up what eventually became the business district of South Liberty Street. During those years, they bought eight other parcels totaling 11.4 acres in the area. Some of these parcels were acquired from white landowners including W. Wash Thompson, sheriff of Spartanburg County, and Joseph Walker, the largest merchant in Spartanburg and partner to Spartan Mills founder John H. Montgomery. The fact that these white men were willing to sell Young land indicates that he was esteemed among whites as well as blacks in Spartanburg. Another tract was purchased from Thomas Pickenpack, a black laborer and father to Phyllis Goins, an important health care worker for whom a housing project was later named.

Young's children prospered, too. According to the white-owned *Carolina Spartan* newspaper, Pierce Butler Young "had bought a lot and built a nice house on Magnolia Street" at the time of his death on June 3, 1884.

❖   ❖   ❖

Before coming to Spartanburg, Joseph Young was a deacon in a Georgia Baptist Church, according to records from the federal Works Progress Administration, and he wanted a Baptist church for his new community in Spartanburg. Most of the black families in the city of Spartanburg at the time attended Methodist churches on the Northside and at Silver Hill. The WPA's *History of Spartanburg County* indicates that Joseph Young was a founder of Mount Moriah Baptist Church. Although records are sketchy, early history indicates that this church began in a brush arbor on the Southside, possibly as early as 1863. Construction of the first church building began around 1877 at the corner of South Liberty and Young streets (named for Joseph Young) on land owned by Joseph Young. By 1884, the church also was home to the first black public school in Spartanburg, Lincoln School, which operated in the basement.

While Mount Moriah was the first Baptist Church in the neighborhood, two others Macedonia Baptist (1894) and Majority Baptist (1902) grew from it, all three with their beginnings on South Liberty Street. Because of that, the name "The Baptistside" was adopted by those who spoke affectionately of the area. "The Baptistside" extended from East Park Avenue to Caulder Avenue, while the larger Southside was bounded by East Main, Collins Avenue, South Liberty, and Duncan streets.

By 1896 the black population of the Southside swelled to several hundred as 125 houses were built in the area around South Liberty Street. Few of these residents appeared in the 1880 city directory (the only directory published prior to 1896), indicating that they had moved to the growing Southside from the countryside, rather than moving across town. Meanwhile, other black homes were built during this period in the backyards of the wealthy white homeowners along South Church Street. Hampton Alley, for instance, was home to many black families who worked as gardeners and housekeepers at the white-owned mansions. Many of the so-called alleys in the neighborhood developed this way, and remained unpaved even into the 1970s. From the first appearance of blacks on the Southside in the 1860s to the years after World War II, blacks and whites often were neighbors, living in close proximity, yet they lived in two different worlds and mixing was a rarity.

Because of the Jim Crow system that institutionalized racial segregation, Southside residents were generally clustered in the low-paying, unskilled occupations open to Southern blacks in the late nineteenth century—laborers, laundresses, drivers, butlers, messengers, and cooks. Nonetheless, some held skilled jobs in the construction trades or professional positions. For example, Fannie Byrd, a teacher, resided at 27 East

This, one of the oldest surviving photos of Southside residents, is Carrie Farrow *(left)* and her sister, Mary, daughters of Lot Farrow. This photograph dates from about 1880. ~Courtesy, Frances Thompson

Valley Street in 1896, and numerous bricklayers and carpenters made their homes in the neighborhood. Carrie Evins, living at 341 Cudd Street, was a nurse, and Edward B. Gregory ran a grocery on South Church Street. Barbers also appeared among the area's African-American residents. A common trade among black men, barbers enjoyed steady employment, relatively high pay, and considerable status in the African-American community.

The Young family remained fixtures in the community at the end of the century. In 1896, Joseph and Priscilla were living at 291 South Liberty Street with their daughter, Mamie, a 30-year-old teacher, and their sons William, a bricklayer, and Edgar, who had no occupation listed in the city directory. Their son Kenneth, a barber, lived nearby at 81 Young Street, while another son, T. Perry Young, also a bricklayer, lived at 306 South Liberty. The Young children likely settled on land owned by their father.

People who would become the twentieth century leaders of Spartanburg's black community joined the Young family on the Southside. Lot Farrow, an emancipated slave who once belonged to the Wilson family on South Church Street, opened a livery stable nearby on Daniel Morgan Avenue. He and his wife, Adeline, gave birth to two of the most important teachers in early black education in Spartanburg: Mary Honor Farrow Wright (1861) and Clara Henry Farrow Young. Mary Wright, who studied at Scotia Seminary and Claflin College before returning home to Spartanburg County to teach, lived at 388 South Liberty Street. Wright and her husband, William, a house painter from York, South Carolina, had ten children, two of whom died in infancy. The Wrights raised their children on the Southside, and in 1904 Mary Wright organized a school in her home for black children who were too young to walk to the nearest black elementary school on Dean Street. This institution eventually became a public school known as the Carrier Street School, and Wright became known as the leading black educator in Spartanburg during her 66-year teaching career. (When Carrier Street School was replaced, the new school was named "Mary H. Wright School" in her honor.)

The wedding photographs of William Wright and Mary H. Farrow in 1884. Mary, who had a 66-year-teaching career in Spartanburg, is 22 years old in this photograph.
~Courtesy, Frances Thompson

Mary H. Wright's children:

- Addie B. McWhirter, born 1885, taught school in Spartanburg
- Willie Wright, born 1887, was a bike mechanic in Spartanburg, then moved to Washington D.C.
- Nina M. Wright., born 1889, was a teacher in Spartanburg
- A set of twins, born in 1891 and died in infancy
- Carrie Nell Hamilton, born 1894, held a government position in Washington. D.C.
- Ruth E. Bridges, born 1896, was a teacher in Spartanburg
- Bennie M. Mansel, born 1898, taught school in Spartanburg
- J. Bratton Wright, born 1899, was a shoemaker in Washington D.C.
- Richard Francis Wright, born 1900, was an undertaker in Boston

Ethel Wood Linder, born in 1902, lived on Caulder Circle and in Tobe Hartwell Apartments. She was one of the first African Americans hired by Spartanburg General Hospital. This photograph was taken in 1916. She died in 1992. ~Courtesy, Beatrice Hill

Clara Farrow, another educational pioneer, established Epiphany Bible School with her sister, Mary. Originally located on Wall Street just off Morgan Square, it moved in 1897 to the new Episcopal mission in the Southside neighborhood. She married Joseph Young's son Perry and they made their home together on South Liberty Street. At her death on April 9, 1905, the *Spartanburg Journal* reported that her funeral "was one of the largest ever held in the city."

The 1905-06 city directory also shows C C. Woodson Sr., another important Spartanburg educator, living on South Liberty Street, a few doors down from community patriarch Joseph Young. Woodson, who married Joseph's youngest daughter, Mamie, was a bricklayer that year, but the next decade he was teaching at the Carrier Street School where he eventually became the principal. Their son, C.C. Woodson Jr., became principal of Carver High in the 1930s.

♦ ♦ ♦

As Spartanburg's black population grew, so did the neighborhood around South Liberty Street. The 1905-06 city directory indicates that South Liberty Street and many of the side streets emanating from it were populated mostly by African Americans. The first side streets to develop were Cudd Street, Young Street, Cemetery Street, and East Valley, followed by Carrier, Rigby, and East Hampton. Whites dominated South Church Street, which was almost entirely residential at the time, but a few blacks lived along that street as well, especially in its 300 block. Two blocks farther south on Church Street was the blacksmith shop of Henry Clemmons, who had lived there since at least 1870.

THE EAST INN
BOARDING AND LODGING

First Class Accommodations, Large, Clean and Comfortable Rooms. Good Table Service And Healthy Location.

When you visit Spartanburg enquire for the East Inn.

Mrs. Mary Wright, Prop.
388 Liberty St., Spartanburg, S. C.

Mary H. Wright operated "The East Inn" in her home at 388 Liberty Street. ~Courtesy, Frances Thompson

While there were few businesses on the Southside at the turn of the century, a black business district was emerging on Morgan Square along Short Wofford Street. Several operators of the early restaurants, barbershops, and butcher shops on Short Wofford were residents of the Southside neighborhood.

Joseph Young died June 2, 1906, just shy of his ninetieth birthday, having outlived at least five of his children. The white-owned *Spartanburg Herald* ran a short obituary, calling him "an industrious and respected Negro." His wife Priscilla died three years later.

By the 1910s and 1920s an increasing number of businesses would open on South Liberty Street, indicating its growing importance to the economic life of the Southside's black residents. Wood Brothers Grocery, W. A. McFee's Grocery, and a half-dozen restaurants were listed on the street by 1916. Some of these businesses were short-lived, but they were soon replaced by other enterprises.

Two of Mary Wright's daughters in a photograph taken soon after the turn of the century. ~Courtesy, Frances Thompson

In the 1920s there were neighborhoods inside of neighborhoods, and most everyone knew everyone else and where they lived. There were Cemetery Street and Cemetery Alley (upper and lower), East Park and East Hampton Avenue, Cut-rate Alley, Dog Hollow, Cudd and East Valley Streets, Clark Street and Clark Alley, Young Street and Young's Alley, Hampton, Rigby, and Martin's Alley. There were Byrd, Pyle, Clements, Celestial, Carrier, Gentry, and Sydney streets.

By the mid-1930s the Southside's black community grew to more than a thousand people. The heart of the neighborhood was South Liberty Street. The growing black business district, Mount Moriah and Majority Baptist Churches, and Carver High School, all important community institutions, were located here. Some blocks in the areas radiating from South Liberty Street—those inhabited by African-American business owners, professionals, or blue-collar workers with steady jobs—maintained remarkable stability throughout the middle decades of the century. Cemetery Street was populated by several people with professional jobs, while teachers congregated on Carrier Street and upper Clement. Blocks inhabited by laborers tended to be more transient— some had high turnover rates ranging from 40 to 80 percent over a five-year period. This turnover not only indicated the lack of economic stability among some Southside residents— it was uncommon to see a laborer live or work in the same place for an extended period of years—but it also it reflected substandard housing on those blocks. Most families who lived in substandard housing were there out of desperation and only until they could find or afford better housing.

Frank Nichols Sr., born in 1911. Nichols was a bricklayer. ~Courtesy, Frank Nichols Jr.

A large number of Southside residents, however, achieved a good level of financial and residential stability, according to a review of Spartanburg city directories. Men who worked as janitors in schools, churches, and businesses or as porters and elevator operators often achieved a measure of economic success, as did men and women with professions and their own businesses. Some women worked as domestics for the same employer for years while others moved from job to job in search of better pay. Illustrating the growing middle class on the Southside, a large percentage of married women stayed home: women who had jobs were teachers and business owners. Many of the residents remained in the same houses and occupied the same jobs year after year, city directories show, while the property ownership rate among the African Americans in the area immediately surrounding South Liberty Street steadily increased.

Most of the black residents occupied blue-collar and service jobs, but a fair number of business owners lived in the area, often above or near their businesses. For example, Nancy Abercrombie, a teacher turned proprietor of the Southside Cafe, lived on Carrier Street, a few blocks away from her business. Teachers from nearby Carver High and Carrier Street Elementary, including

The home of Dr. William Douglas on South Liberty Street ~Courtesy, Jacqualine D. Farr

Nancy Abercrombie's husband, John, Emma G. Reeder, and Azalee McGee, lived in the area as well. A number of insurance agents also lived in the neighborhood, including McKinley Muckelduff, an agent for Pilgrim Health and Life (who later became manager of Tobe Hartwell apartments in the 1940s). Black physician William S. Douglas lived and practiced on the lower end of South Liberty. He lived in one of several middle-class homes along South Liberty, many with wraparound porches and shiny wooden floors.

In the mid to late 1930s several people still lived in the neighborhood who had grown up under slavery. When interviewers from the Federal Writers Project

J. Bratton Wright *(left)* born in 1899, was the second son of Mary and William Wright. This photograph dates from about 1915. His companion is unidentified. ~Courtesy, Frances Thompson

came through the Southside in the summer of 1937, they found at least four former slaves willing to share their memories. Among these were "Aunt" Annie Gallman, 84, and Mary Williams, who lived in the "Old Ladies Home" at 391 Cudd Street. Mrs. Williams recounted the story of seeing Yankee soldiers marching through town during the Civil War. Ninety-year-old "Uncle" Jimmie Johnson, who lived at 172 East Park Avenue, told of attending the white Episcopal Church of the Advent as a slave and remembered Yankee soldiers taking sugar and ham from the home of his Spartanburg slavemaster. Another ex-slave, Govan Littlejohn, 87, lived at 387 Liberty Street.

Descendents of Joseph Young continued to reside on the Southside. Joseph's youngest son, Charles, was a barber who owned a home on South Liberty Street. Another son, bricklayer T. Perry, also continued to live on that street near his brother (and fellow bricklayer) Henry. Joseph's son Kenneth lived on South Liberty as well. According to the city directories and the 1920 census, Kenneth was a mail carrier. The fact that he held a federal appointment in the Jim Crow era was indicative of his stature among local whites as well as blacks. Later Youngs, many of them the grandchildren of Joseph, continued to live in the neighborhood, run businesses, and teach school.

By the 1940s several places for home-cooked meals had become established in the area. Lillie Howard's Cafe was known for delicious meals of fresh vegetables and meats. Po Boy's Lunch, operated by the family of Jim Reynolds, was said to have the best fish sandwiches. Liza Ellis made what many considered the best sweet potato pies. By the early 1950s the Southside Cafe was opened by Nancy Abercrombie, a former teacher. She prepared fresh vegetables daily and served full-course meals. (The bologna sandwiches were many people's favorite.) The Southside was also a favorite stop for ice cream lovers.

Until mid-century, whites and blacks co-existed on the periphery of the South Liberty Street area—Caulder and Carrier Streets to the south, South Church Street to the west, and the northern reaches of South Liberty itself—but gradually whites moved out of this section of the Southside. South Church Street

Bootsie Campbell *(right)* and a friend in Tobe Hartwell, 1950
~Courtesy, the Moss and Campbell families

gradually became a commercial district while black residents replaced whites on the other streets. A Texaco service station appeared at 611 South Church in the early 1960s. By the end of the decade, a self-service laundry, a fish market, a dry cleaner, and a radio/TV repair shop had opened nearby.

As whites moved out, large homes were converted to apartment buildings or new apartment complexes were built. African Americans moved into these newly renovated homes. For example, in 1952 the city directory lists the Belena Apartments at the corner of South Church and Clement Street in a location once occupied by a single-family dwelling. A similar apartment house appeared at 427 South Church Street by the late 1950s. The Spartanburg Housing Authority broke ground on September 10, 1940, for Tobe Hartwell Courts on Clement Street, the first public housing project in Spartanburg and a prestigious address for its first 150 black families. Additional apartments were added in 1952.

A study of Spartanburg city directories reveals that many of the Southside neighborhood's residents achieved some upward economic mobility over the years in spite of the limited employment opportunities available to African Americans. For example, Carl Ellis, at 430 Wade Street, was listed as a laborer in the 1943-44 city directory, but by 1958 he was in business for himself as a coal vendor.

✧   ✧   ✧

The South Liberty Street business district grew over the course of the century as well. In the 1930s the street was primarily residential, but by 1940

South Liberty had been transformed into the commercial center of the community. Beauty shops, barber shops, cafes, pawn shops, billiard parlors, liquor stores, and repair shops lined South Liberty Street and were present on side streets as well.

Professionals also set up shop on South Liberty Street. In the 1950s Whaley's Pharmacy opened on South Liberty Street and was soon joined by Bull's Clinic. Lawyer Matthew J. Perry, soon to be a noted civil rights lawyer and judge, had offices over Dr. Bull's Clinic in the late 1950s and early 1960s. By this time, Whaley's Pharmacy had changed to Oliver's Pharmacy and was operated by Dr. Edwin Oliver. North Carolina Mutual Insurance, an insurance company that catered to black customers, occupied an office at 375 South Liberty, between Bull's Clinic and Oliver's Pharmacy in the early 1950s. Several mortuaries served the neighborhood and indeed blacks from all over Spartanburg County; Abrams and Hayes, and Wood Mortuary were among the first ones, followed by E. L. Collins, Dawkins and Smith, and later, Craig and Thompson.

Businesses appeared on some of the side streets off South Liberty as well, and often houses were converted to businesses and then back to residential use. For example, at 568 Martins Alley white businessman Roy D. Fowler owned a grocery store that served the community. By 1940 the grocery store had been replaced by Dawkins Beer Garden, a beer retailer owned by black businessman Norman Dawkins. Eight years later, the business was being run by his brother,

A shot of Young Street in 1947
~Courtesy,
Margaret Finley

A view of the western side of South Liberty Street from the entrance of Collins Funeral Home. Dr. George T. Mansel's office is on the left, and Mrs. Nina Wright's house is on the right.
~Courtesy, Kitty Collins Tullis

Roland Dawkins. The site was later occupied by the Cozy Inn Cafe and Dawkins Night Club, both operated by Roland Dawkins, and by 1968 it became home to the Church of the Living God, a storefront church. Fowler's Grocery moved from Martins Alley to Young Street and became Johnny's Food Fair. By the 1960s Oliver's Pharmacy had a lunch counter and a soda fountain and had become a favorite hangout for teens after a Carver football or basketball game. Collins Hotel, also located on South Liberty, was the only place where black entertainers and others could stay when coming to Spartanburg.

In the early 1940s James Herrington Young (unrelated to the Joseph Young family) moved to

Barbara *(left)* and Ann Montgomery with Ed Rochell, Spartanburg's first black painting contractor. This photo was taken at 177 Young Street in 1943.
~Courtesy, Barbara Collier

Vincent Foster at age 2 on East Valley Street with Shepard Richards
~Courtesy, Therlon Joyner

Spartanburg from Columbia with his wife, Octavia, and his daughter, Annie Young Gordon. A stonemason and bricklayer by profession, he purchased property on Liberty Street, which he rented out to a laundromat, liquor store, and a church. He later built a food store on Cemetery Street.

The South Liberty Street area was home to a number of community institutions as well. Besides the schools and churches, there was the Spartan Star Lodge No. 108 of the Ancient Free and Accepted Masons; a Catholic Mission for the Colored, which was located on East Hampton Avenue for a brief time during the 1940s before moving to Duncan Street; a U.S. Army Aid Station, a place where war veterans went for assistance; and a USO for Camp Croft soldiers.

The west side of the neighborhood, the area centered on South Liberty Street, was the heart of the Southside's African-American community, but a significant number of black people also lived on the neighborhood's east side, the area between the point where Cemetery Street took a sharp southeastern turn and Union Street. Here blacks and whites lived on adjacent blocks. In the late 1940s and early 1950s whites began to move out of the blocks closest to Liberty Street, but many of the blocks closest to Union Street remained predominantly or completely white until the 1970s.

A review of the city directories tells a story of population growth in the eastern portion of the Southside neighborhood. In the 1930s some blocks in the area were vacant, but single-family homes were built there in the 1940s and 1950s. Usually whites from both white-collar and blue-collar families moved into the new homes. However, by the late 1950s or early 1960s many of the houses in this area were converted from single-family residences to multi-family apartment houses or boarding houses. New apartment houses were also constructed. Many widows remained in their homes after the death of a spouse but began to take in boarders. Much of the eastern Southside experienced significant turnover during the mid-1960s. For example, 90 percent of the homes in the block bordered by Marion Avenue, South Converse Street, Bomar Street, and Winsmith Street changed hands between 1962 and 1968. The same area saw an 80 percent turnover rate between 1968 and 1972. Even blocks inhabited by whites saw a decline in the socioeconomic status of residents, as evidenced by both occupational categories and home ownership rates.

For example, by 1952, though the residents of Marion Avenue remained white, the majority had become renters. The turnover rate, the socioeconomic downturn among residents, and the rise of multi-family housing in this area suggest that properties there may have deteriorated as the neighborhood began to decline. Nonetheless, most of the east side of the Southside neighborhood lay outside the designated clearance area for urban renewal, and the houses here were not leveled in the mid-1970s. The houses were later rented or sold to African Americans.

Carolyn Cheeks and Deb Bonds sit on the hood of a car in 1957 on Sydney Street.
~Courtesy, Irene Bonds

Other blocks on the neighborhood's eastern edge demonstrated stable residential patterns over time. For example, the blocks around Freeman's Cemetery, a historic black cemetery later known as Cemetery Street Cemetery, were stable, with many African-American extended family groups settling there for decades. Members of the Byrd, Beatty, Chapman, Evans, and Bethea families appeared on these blocks throughout the first three-quarters of the twentieth century. A substantial number of households adjacent to the cemetery were headed by women, not the predominant pattern in the Southside throughout its existence.

Though most of the eastern blocks of Southside were residential, a few businesses began to spring up along Union Street by the 1960s. Gilstrap Drug Company at 508 Union Street appeared in the city directory in 1958 and in the late 1960s was replaced with King's OK Tire Store. The Letter Shop, a printing business, was established on a long-vacant property at 480 Union Street in 1968.

By the late 1960s some of the older buildings on the Southside were on the decline, but the neighborhood remained a thriving and closely-knit community

The northwest corner of East Henry and South Liberty streets, 1967. The building is Lamb's Grocery.
~Courtesy, Spartanburg County Regional Museum of History

with a number of established institutions and extended families who had settled near each other. The steady growth of the business district, as evidenced by information from city directories, is one indicator of the vitality of the neighborhood. But the vivid memories of its residents—and emotional witness some 50 years later—are perhaps the best evidence of the significance of that time and place.

◇ *Researched and written by—*
- *The Hub City Writers Project: Betsy Teter, Melissa Walker, Beatrice Hill, and Brenda Lee*
- *Melissa Walker's fall 2004 African-American history class at Converse College: Kim Anderson, Jeff Callis, Michael Colebank, Heather Couch, Sheila Davis, Amy Driggers, David Eaton, Jennifer Gray, Angela Haney, David Kelly, Douglas King, Libby Long, Elizabeth Ann Moore, Katherine Morrison, Kimberly Newton, Merry Poore, Elizabeth Sloughter, Traci Taylor and Michael Tumblin.*

Obituaries of Prominent African-American Residents

While the deaths of black Spartanburg residents were not routinely reported in white-owned newspapers until the 1950s, these early citizens did receive small notices.

Lot Farrow
April 1, 1885

Lot Farrow, the most industrious colored citizen we had, died Monday night. The general impression was that it was hard constant work that killed him. Day and night, if necessary, he pushed ahead with his drays, and cold or hot, wet or dry, he was at work. Such industry is rare. He gave his children a good education and brought them up to be respected and respectable.
—*The Carolina Spartan*

Clara Farrow Young
April 11, 1906

   The funeral of Clara Young, wife of Perry Young, a well known colored man, was held this afternoon, her death having occurred Sunday morning. The funeral was one of the largest ever held in the city. The deceased was one of the best colored women in the city.
   She was highly respected, well educated, having received her education at Orangeburg. During her life she put the advantages she had received to good use in this city for she engaged in teaching the colored children of Spartanburg. Perry Young, the husband of the deceased, is a member of one of the oldest and best known colored families in the city. He is a brickmason, hard working and honest and bears the goodwill and friendship of all classes of people, white and colored.
   Just before the hour for the funeral today, a number of white people from prominent families in the city called at the house of the deceased woman and left floral offerings.
—*The Spartanburg Journal*

Joseph Young
June 3, 1906

   Joseph Young, colored, died at his home, 294 South Liberty Street, yesterday at the advanced age of 89. He would have been 90 years old in a few months. He was an industrious and respected negro; a mattress maker by trade.
—*The Carolina Spartan*

☆2

Early Residents

"Coming down (South Liberty Street) on the right there were homes of people like Mary H. Wright, Dr. Mansel, the Young brothers and their families. Those people had the nice, big two-story homes with yards full of trees."

—Harriet Dawkins

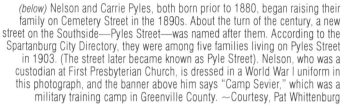

(below) Nelson and Carrie Pyles, both born prior to 1880, began raising their family on Cemetery Street in the 1890s. About the turn of the century, a new street on the Southside—Pyles Street—was named after them. According to the Spartanburg City Directory, they were among five families living on Pyles Street in 1903. (The street later became known as Pyle Street). Nelson, who was a custodian at First Presbyterian Church, is dressed in a World War I uniform in this photograph, and the banner above him says "Camp Sevier," which was a military training camp in Greenville County. ~Courtesy, Pat Whittenburg

The two photos above are some of the earliest residents of the Southside area. Joseph Sims changed his name to Joseph Evans after being freed from slavery. He married Mary Rice, pictured here, and they lived at 378 Cemetery Street, directly across from the neighborhood cemetery. ~Courtesy, Cynthia Scruggs

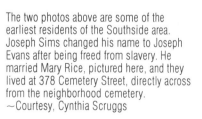

> *"The doctors visited the homes when I was a little girl. I remember Dr. Hardy and there was Dr. Sexton who operated a drug store on South Church Street, one block from Main Street, known as Sexton's Drug Store. In the rooms above Dr. Sexton was the office of our first black dentist. His name was Dr. G. K. Adams. At that time there was no other hospital for us. Later there was another hospital on Howard Street, known as the Providence Hospital. It was operated by a Mrs. Carrie Bomar who later became Mrs. Carrie Perry."*
>
> —Harriet Dawkins

(left) Carrie Pyles. Carrie was sister to Mary Evans, who married early Southside resident and former slave, Joseph Evans ~Courtesy, Pat Whittenburg

(right) Lannie Pyles, late 1920s or early 1930s. She married Rome Pyles and they lived at 501 Byrd Street about the time of this photograph. ~Courtesy, Pat Whittenburg

Frank Nichols Sr. was a member of one of the earliest families living on the Southside. His grandfather, Jefferson, a farmer, appears in the 1896 City Directory at 28 Cudd Street. Jefferson's son, Green, married Ophelia, who gave birth to Frank Nichols Sr. in 1911. Frank Sr. was a bricklayer on the Southside, as was his son, Frank Jr. ~Courtesy, Frank Nichols

Ernest Coln, who lived on Clement Street, was the youngest of educator Hannah Coln's nine children. He worked at the Ritz Theater and is the grandfather of Brenda Lee. ~Courtesy, Brenda Lee

Mamie Green Anderson, mother of Althea Amos
~Courtesy, Brenda Lee

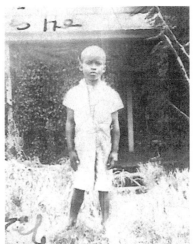

The photograph, taken about 1930, shows Willie B. Wilson Jr. at his house in "Dog Hollow," an area between Cudd and Cemetery Streets. Wilson was born in 1922. ~Courtesy, Beatrice Hill

Maude Wilson, born in 1901. This photo is from 1918. ~Courtesy, Beatrice Hill

Willie B. Wilson Sr., born in 1898, lived on Cemetery Street. He was a World War I veteran who fought in Mexico. He played the bugle for the U.S. Army. This photo is from 1918. ~Courtesy, Beatrice Hill

This photograph from the turn of the century shows Nora Bagwell Long and Tom Long at their home at 190 South Dean Street. Nora was born into slavery on the Bagwell Plantation, which was located off Country Club Road about where Oak Creek Plantation is today. After emancipation, she became a nurse for Stanyarne Wilson (a white Spartanburg lawyer and state senator) and also worked at Converse College for a period. She raised Ada Bagwell Foster, who became principal of Dean Street School. ~Courtesy, Rosalind Brown

This photograph of Effie Parks is from the Rosalind Patton Brown photo collection. Miss Parks appears in the 1918 Spartanburg City Directory as a laborer living at 275 Young Street.

"My stepmother was a laundry lady. That is how we made our living, by laundering there at home. We had the Octagon soap and we had the lye soap that was made from the grease that was saved up from frying bacon or other meats and sage lye. The soap was made in a wash pot. We'd boil the clothes, and used a stick to lift the clothes from the bottom of the pot to the top, to make sure all of them got a chance to boil real good killing all the germs. There would be three big tin tubs: when you took the clothes from the wash pot to number one, then number two was clear water for rinse and number three for bluing, which made them snow white. There was no Clorox at that time. The bluing came in a box with five sticks in it, costing five cents. There were only three ways that my people had of making an honest living back then. You would launder clothes in your home, go to the cotton patch, or go to the cook kitchen."

—Harriet Dawkins

Members of the Wright and Farrow families dressed for church. This photo was taken in the early 1900s.
~Courtesy, Frances Thompson

(above) In the early 1920s Eugene Goodlett served as manager of a meat market in the first block of South Liberty Street. The market was owned by Clarence Pettit, who was white. Goodlett lived at 184 South Dean Street in 1922. ~Courtesy, Rosalind Brown

Carrie Nell Wright Hamilton, born in 1894, was the third daughter of Mary H. Wright. ~Courtesy, Frances Thompson

Bratton Wright, Mary Wright's son. This photo dates from the 1920s. ~Courtesy, Frances Thompson

Farrow Belle McWhirter, daughter of Addie B. Wright McWhirter, was Mary H. Wright's granddaughter. Farrow Belle lived many years with her mother and was instrumental in the restoration of the Cemetery Street Cemetery on the Southside.
~Courtesy, Frances Thompson

Bennie Mae Wright, born in 1898, was the fifth daughter of Mary and William Wright. She taught typing in a building near Short Wofford and Saint John Streets. She married Dr. George Mansel, who became the resident physician of the Southside.
~Courtesy, Frances Thompson

Joe Patton was born in 1914 in an area near Oakwood Cemetery. He married Fordham Foster and in 1937 they moved to the Southside, in a home at the corner of South Dean and Henry streets. He served as the barber in the Southside for many years. ~Courtesy, Rosalind Brown

Benjamin and Maggie Ferguson came to the Southside around the 1920s. In the early 1930s they lived on East Hampton Avenue, and Benjamin is listed in the Spartanburg City Directory as a laborer. Their daughter, Lannie, married Rome Pyles. ~Courtesy, Pat Whittenburg

Lannie Pyles, late 1920s or early 1930s. She married Rome Pyles and they lived at 501 Byrd Street about the time of this photograph. ~Courtesy, Pat Whittenburg

"Dupré Book Store was where the schools got their books, but ... very few black children could afford to buy new books. After about four years the new books from the white schools were traded in for more new ones, and the used ones were sent to the black schools. My mother and I did the laundry for Mr. Cavis, who was the manager of Dupré Book Store, and he would always ask my mother if I passed my grade; then he would save new books for me, so I was fortunate enough not to have to get used books."

—Harriet Dawkins

Some children from the Southside attended Cumming Street School near Wofford College. In this photograph from the 1920s, Southside businessman Ernest Collins is in the top row, third boy from the left, wearing a dark tie.
~Courtesy, Kitty Collins Tullis

« 29 »

3

Memories of the Neighborhood

❝We usually had our fun going to
the ten-cent shimmy rent parties.
There were two brothers, Willie and
Walt Fuller—they could really play
the heck out of a piano—and that was
our music, they could play anything.
Most of the time wherever the party
was, there was a piano, and the
Fuller brothers would be there.❞

—Willie B. Wilson, Jr.

Harriet Dawkins

(courtesy, Raymond Floyd)

Harriet Dawkins was born in 1907 near the lower end of Glendalyn Avenue, on Saint Paul Street, about where the YMCA is now. As a young girl she moved to the Southside with her family and grew up on Carrier Street. Mary H. Wright and Fannie Young were her elementary school teachers. She was 97 years old at the time of this 2004 interview, when she walked her visitors up and down South Liberty Street with memories that date as far back as 1915.

There was, starting on the corner of Clement Street and South Liberty, a house and a grocery store called Willis Perry's Store, which later became Abrams and Hayes Funeral Home. Next was Mr. Henry Perry's residence, who was an attorney, [who] had a brick building on his property and it was called Perry's Hotel. Now, there was the home of Ms. Mary Carter, then Ms. Claudia Moore, and then Mr. Rossi and Mrs. Ruby Sexton, and there was Selima Jackson who had a building and rented to Abernathy Grocery Store, and Mr. Andrew Prysock ran the shoe repair shop, then [there was] the parsonage and Mount Moriah Baptist Church.

On the corner of Young Street (named after Mr. Joe Young, the grandfather of C.C. Woodson Jr.) and Liberty Street was a restaurant operated by Rosa and Walsh Reynolds where they sold hot fish sandwiches and sweet potato custards for about 15 or 20 cents each. Much similar to the drive-in of today, only back then you walked instead of driving. You come in, order, paid and picked it up when it was ready and left— there were no facilities for eating on the premises.

Next, in a small building, there was a Mr. Dale who ran a pot-mending business. He repaired pots and pans for people—that shop later became a place called Mattees, and later a shoeshine parlor. Going on up was another restaurant ran by Lewis Haynes and Bob and Carrie Sims; it was much like the buffet style of today. Later there was a small golf course with lights, added on in the back, somewhat like the putt-putt golf of today. Years later Mrs. Hattie Barksdale (niece of Lewis Haynes) ran the business. This building was torn down and years later, in the same spot, was a movie house called the Liberty Theater, that later became the Southside Cafe, operated by Mrs. Abercrombie.

A Mr. [Thomas] Bomar owned a store in the next building, and he also owned stock in one of the local cotton mills [Spartan Mills], which was unheard of back then for a black man. The next building on the corner of Cemetery and Liberty Streets was the Sam Foster Store. Now, crossing Cemetery going towards East Valley Street there was another store on the corner. In the next two houses there are persons who did hair in their homes; they were Bessie Richards and Clara Fant.

Between East Valley Street and Hampton Avenue were only two buildings, the home of Mr. C.C. Woodson (who was principal for many years at Carver High) and the Majority Baptist Church. Still traveling upward, on the corner of Liberty and Hampton was a building that stayed empty most of the time. Next there was a barbershop called Jim Twitty's Barbershop. Another gentleman known as Mr. Shavers operated another little eating place where you could get peanuts and hot fish sandwiches, and next to him was the Real Cafe. It was operated by Mrs. Leila Howard.

I had gone on the inside with someone else, and it was really something back then, because she had about four tables where you could sit down and eat. Mrs. Leila Howard had some of the best home-cooked food around. Next, a house that sat a little off the street was the parish house that was next to the Epiphany Church. At that time it was called the Episcopal Mission. It was there that the first black private school began. The principal was also the rector of the Episcopal Church—his name was Bagwell—and of course the school was called Bagwell School. There were quite a number of students that attended there who were a bit older than I at that time because I was only about eight or nine years old then.

Next to the church was a miniature golf course. I didn't know too much about it then, but that property belonged to Mr. Floyd Wood. His home sat a ways back off the street. Mr. Wood purchased a large building on the same lot, and it became the Floyd Wood Funeral Home. He operated the funeral home until his wife died, then sold it to E. L. Collins. The building on the corner he rented out to a firm that introduced new products—it was there that I heard of Clorox for the first time. That firm also sold some sort of cola and fruity drink.

Crossing Park Avenue on the corner of Liberty was the property of the Williams family, who [later] sold to Dr. Bull for his clinic on the ground level and a barbershop in a lower level on one side operated by Mr. Joe Patton, and an apartment on the other side, that years later became a photographer's studio run by Odell Young.

As we go farther up Liberty toward downtown, there was a Sphinx Hotel facing Broad Street that was white-owned, and they carried newspapers from different states. There were black soldiers in Camp Wadsworth that were from the Northern states, and they wanted to read the newspaper from their hometown. The only place they could find that particular paper was in the lobby of the Sphinx Hotel, and of course in those days it caused quite an uproar when they proceeded to go into the lobby to purchase the paper.

Traveling out Broad Street to the corner of South Church Street was the business of Mr. Charlie Bomar and his son, Joe Bomar, and Joe Young, son of Mr. Joe Young Sr. They had a shoe repair business with the entrance on South Church Street. Coming down Church Street on the same side between Broad and Kennedy Streets, was Sexton's Drugstore, operated by Dr. Sexton, father of Helen Gray and Lula Abrams, who in later years, were teachers at Carver High School. The first time I saw wrought iron chairs was at Dr. Sexton's Drugstore.

Coming back to Liberty Street, going down across the street from Bull's Clinic but up a ways, was a cleaner. That is what we called them back then because you could drop your clothes off there and they would clean them, much like the dry cleaner of today. That building later became home to several businesses like a barbershop, a Masonic lodge, and a nightclub.

Coming down on the right there were homes of people like Mary H. Wright, Dr. Mansel, the Young brothers and their families. Those people had the nice, big two-story homes with yards full of trees. A building on the edge of the yard on the corner of Hampton Avenue and South Liberty Street was once used for boarders, and later rented to Mrs. Lilly Reed for a store, where she sold grocery items, ice cream, and snowballs. Now crossing Hampton on the corner was an eating place and an entertaining place called the Blue Lantern. Going down about two blocks was another establishment that was built for a shoe repair shop, run by Ernest Daniel and Joe Young—it later became Dawkins and Smith Funeral Home operated by Mr. Norman Dawkins.

—*Interview by Beatrice Hill, Brenda Lee, and Betsy Teter*

(courtesy, Raymond Floyd)

Madge Young Williams

Born in 1910 in Laurens County, Madge Young Williams came to Spartanburg about 1922 to be a boarding student at the private Cedar Hill Academy. Cedar Hill was the only school in the area for black children that went all the way to the 11th grade. She graduated in 1929 and became a teacher in Greenville and Laurens counties. In an interview from 2004, she shares her memories of Cedar Hill.

My father was a farmer who owned his farm of 90 acres. My mother and my three brothers helped him with that. I was the youngest, and the only girl, so I didn't have to go out into the fields and work, but I did have to take them water, fix their lunch, and do the dishes. I attended Cedar Hill Academy in Spartanburg in the sixth grade. Cedar Hill was a big two-story building. The classrooms were on the ground floor, and the girls' dormitory was up above that. There was an extension added on for the kitchen and dining area, and the boy's dormitory was above that part. There was a big heater in the halls that heated up the rooms. …

We all had chores to do. Cleaning the halls, our rooms, the kitchen, washing dishes, and there were the big wash pots out back for doing the laundry. When I first arrived there, my mother saw how everyone was working, and said I was too young to work like that, so she packed me enough clothes for a month, then brought more and picked up the dirty ones. I don't think we had a janitor there because the students did all the work. The teachers were Ms. McGee, Mr. and Mrs. Brewton, his sister, Ms. Mamie Brewton, and Reverend Earle, the principal.

Reverend Earle was pastor at Mount Moriah Baptist Church, and all of the boarding students had to attend Sunday school, church, and BTU services. I was the only boarding student that joined Mount Moriah, but I did it through Watch Care, because I still had my membership with my home church, and I joined the YWA, so whenever the church had something, we were not allowed to go anywhere alone, so they would send someone to walk with me so I could participate. This created a little bit of jealousy among the others, because I'd get to go off campus more than they did. While I was at Cedar Hill, I had an appendectomy, and the surgery was done at a hospital on Howard Street.

When I reached high school, I could sing back then, and Reverend Earle had a quartet of girls, and we would travel from place to place doing programs to raise money for the school. I did solos, and there was a girl from Greer who was good at reciting poetry, and she did that. I don't remember any of the songs I sang then, but for graduation I sang "The Indian Love Call." Whenever we went to town, we would cross Liberty Street and walk over to South Church Street and go that way because there were trees for shade while walking. Every year we'd walk from Cedar Hill to the fairgrounds and didn't think anything of the distance. We'd just go and have a good time.

The boarding students always went in a group. I don't think we had to have a teacher with us, as long as we had a group. Cedar Hill had students coming from all over, there was a young man from Tryon, and he lived on campus. There were people who lived in Spartanburg that came every day but didn't live on campus. Parents of the boarding students were always sending boxes of food. I had an uncle Richard Young, who was a blacksmith over behind the jailhouse in Spartanburg, and he would always bring boxes of food for me.

On Friday evenings, we would play games, but we weren't allowed to dance. I remember the May Day activities, and Ms. McGee would play the piano for us, and whenever we'd have a program to do, she'd play for us. Mr. Wright from Mount Moriah had a scout troop, and they used to march up and down the street by the school, and we'd watch from the windows. I knew Rossi D. Sexton and Lucius High who were in the troop because they went to Cedar Hill. It was said back then that Majority was a pull-out from Mount Moriah, and if you went to one, you couldn't bother with the other, but they're better about that now.

I don't remember a lot about Liberty Street because as a student in Cedar Hill, we weren't allowed to roam about, and most of Liberty Street was off limits to us. But I do remember Carrier Street, because our school cook and Ms. McGee lived there; there were the Drakes, who lived across from the school on Liberty Street. They had a beautiful home. There were other families on that street with nice homes, but I don't remember who they were, and, you know, they just tore those houses down.

—*Interview by Beatrice Hill and Brenda Lee*

Curtis "Brother" Foster

Curtis Foster, born in 1922, was the youngest son of the late Ora L. Foster who taught at the Episcopal Epiphany Mission school and, later, in Spartanburg city schools. He grew up in the Liberty Heights area of the Southside, on Appian Drive. An electrician by trade, he is a retired veteran of the U.S. Air Force.

The first store was operated by Reverend Earle and my father. It was on the corner of Cemetery Street and Liberty. They lost that store, and it became Cromer's Grocery. A Mr. C.C. Bomar built a duplex-type building on the opposite corner, and one side became Sam Foster Store, and George

Miller had an ice cream parlor on the other side operated by his son, "Hurry George" we called him. He died about 1929. His widow married Mr. Lipscomb whose house on Liberty faced Clark Street.

Next was a filling station and garage called Allen's Garage, with ten-gallon glass tanks on top of the pumps. At that time Spartanburg was not progressing at all, especially for the blacks, and Mr. Allen decided to leave town. He founded the Spartanburg Sluggers baseball team that went to Newt Whitmire when he left.

Caldwell's Meat Market was below Mr. Lipscomb's house—they sold the *Palmetto Leader* newspaper there that later went to Columbia—then it became a restaurant operated by Lewis Haynes with a golf course next to it, and much later the Southside Cafe, operated by Nancy Abercrombie.

At that time we had three dentists, Dr. Walker, Dr. Young, and Dr. Glymph. The Providence Hospital was operated by Dr. Hardy and Carrie Perry. That building later became the J. W. Woodward Funeral Home. The John Nina Hospital that later became M. S. Callahan Funeral Home was owned and operated by Nina Littlejohn, wife of businessman Worth Littlejohn. Today it is called Callahan and Hicks Funeral Home.

At one time the public school for blacks didn't go any further than the ninth grade; if you wanted to go to the eleventh grade, you would have to go to the Episcopal, the Presbyterian, or to Cedar Hill [schools], because they went to the eleventh grade. In those days the Presbyterians were more interested in education for the black students.

Cedar Hill Academy [located where Mary H. Wright Elementary School now sits] was a private boarding and day school for blacks with grades going to the eleventh grade which originated from Laurens, South Carolina, and was sponsored by the Tiger River Association. It was run by Reverend J. S. Earle and Mr. Holloman, Zack Holloman's father. Mr. Brewton was the first principal, then Mr. Dendy, and later Mr. Goudlock who soon left and convinced several teachers to go with him to Clinton Junior College in Rock Hill. By that time, Cedar Hill was on the decline and was later burned down. Admission was only about fifty cents a week, which was a lot of money back then. In 1929 Brewton went to Cumming Street High, and died shortly after. Cumming Street High was built in 1926, and the first graduating class was in 1929. It was built right next to the Spartanburg incinerator, and the colored hospital [was] right up the street, which spoke of how the blacks were treated back then.

In later years the city of Spartanburg bought and demolished the [Morris] Preston home and built the USO building for the black soldiers at Camp Croft in the early 1940s. That building, still owned by the city, later became the Woodward Recreation Center for the black community. The area on South Church Street where Pete's Barbershop now sits was once owned by my great uncle, Charlie McKinsey, who was of the white race. Practically all of the property below Milster Street in that block belonged to the McKinsey, Mills (as in Reverend George Mills), and the Marshall families, who were black.

South Liberty Street was the main artery coming into the black neighborhoods on the south side of town. Starting point was from the corner of Lee and Liberty Street, with the schoolyard of Jenkins Junior High on the other corner. From that point down it was colored. It was also at that point where the pavement stopped—until 1926, when the rest of Liberty was paved down to Carrier Street. All the paved streets were brick instead of asphalt at that time.

There were streetcars that went all the way to Glenn Springs. There was some sort of resort hotel there, and you'd hear of people coming from all over to visit there. We had the trains—in fact, the old station in east Spartanburg is still there today. I remember trying to help keep the old Majority Church and maybe turn it into a museum or something.

I remember my dad helping to build Majority Church [and] the Episcopal school where the Parish House now sits on part of the property. The school was a big two-story house where the rector and his family lived in one side, and the school was in the other side. At that time, blacks were more cooperative with each other. Now, segregation might have forced it, but the only people who acquired anything then were the teachers, lawyers, and the brick masons. At that time the brick masons were Floyd Wood, Henry Drake, Henry Clemmons, Henry Perry, Sam Foster, Sam Collins, and the Pickenpack brothers.

The Dew Drop Inn was where Arthur Herndon had his candy company. The tall wooden structure sat just a ways off the street at the bottom of Wofford Street next to the underpass and across the street from what is now

Wakefield Buick. Some of the candies he made were peppermint, and my favorite was the peanut butter candy. His distribution was worldwide because most of his salesmen were white, and so was his clientele.

John Coleman and his brother started the Blue Lantern on Liberty Street. There used to be blue lights in the windows, and that is where the name came from. They had a sister named Sadie Coleman. The Blue Lantern sat on the corner of Hampton Avenue and South Liberty Street. A small portion of the building was where Dr. Porter had his drugstore.

—Interview by Beatrice Hill and Brenda Lee

(courtesy, Raymond Floyd)

Cora Byrd Taylor

Cora Byrd was born on Cemetery Street, June 20, 1921. She attended Carrier Street School through the sixth grade, Dean Street School for one year, and then came back to Carver until graduation in the eleventh grade. She attended Spartanburg Methodist College for a year, and then married George Taylor. She helped out at the family business, Caldwell's Grocery, on South Liberty Street, and became one of three black crossing guards for the city of Spartanburg. She is mother to Barbara and to Precious Taylor, who became one of the two first black female police officers in Spartanburg.

George [Taylor] and I grew up two doors from each other, and we had a good neighborhood. At that time your neighbor could chastise you if you did anything wrong, and when your parents got home, they took over. I remember I had to do a day's work before I went to school in the morning, and after school I could play for about an hour, then I had to come in and cook supper. My mother was sick, and I had to fill in. My older sister stayed sick, so I had to do her chores. I was the middle child. There were two sisters and two brothers.

I have lived on the Southside all of my life. When I was growing up we had a good time, boys and girls growing up together. We went out and dated, but we knew how to act, and we had nice clean fun. When our parents told us to be back at a certain time, we were there. Like most parents, they wanted us to have a good education. Even though I got married before finishing college, I had a good husband who was a good provider, and we lived together 52 years before he died.

Being one of the first four black women hired by the city of Spartanburg, I worked as a crossing guard for 16 years. Because of the arthritis in my knees, the doctor told me to get in out of the weather, so I went inside Mary H. Wright and worked there for 39 years. I had met quite a few good friends there. A couple of them were Mrs. Jones and Ella Poats, who raised roses. When my husband started to get sick, I retired and came home to be with him.

We were raised during the time when you had plenty to eat, and what few clothes you had, you kept them clean. I remember one year when I didn't have but two dresses; I'd wear one and wash one, and by the end of the school year the dresses were white as snow, because I had washed all the color out. When I did the laundry, and hung them on the clothesline, if there was a piece that was not right, my mother would take it down and make me do it over, so I learned to do things right the first time.

Liberty Street was a black street, because every business in our area was black, and we had loads of them. There were the funeral homes, churches, restaurants, and Po Boy's had the best hamburgers and hotdogs you ever tasted. I remember Caldwell Meat Market. There was Lewis Haynes who had a building with the restaurant downstairs and a dance floor upstairs—the soldiers would come to town and dance. Now, that was the place to be back then! It was nice. On up the street Mrs. Ellis had a place to eat. The mother of a classmate of mine lived a little farther up, and she had a real nice home.

There were black people that had some lovely homes along Liberty Street.

Not too far from the school was the home of Mrs. Lou Miles—before Dr. William Douglas built his home, everyone knew her as a midwife. She was the type of person that would try almost anything, like riding on the fire truck, stuff like that. Then there was Mrs. Leila Howard up near the kindergarten. She could really cook good food, and she kept order in there—you couldn't go in fooling around. Mrs. Young, who ran the kindergarten, lived across the street.

—Interview by Beatrice Hill

(courtesy, Raymond Floyd)

Constance Brown Manyfield

Constance Brown Manyfield was born in 1926 in Lexington County where her father was the rector of Saint Anne Episcopal Church. When she was six weeks old, he transferred to the Church of the Epiphany on South Liberty Street and the family came to Spartanburg to live in the parsonage. Later they moved to East Valley Street. Connie retired after many years of service from the South Carolina School for the Deaf and the Blind, where she was supervisor of the blind department.

We lived in the church parsonage which was bordered by the church on one side and Mrs. Leila Howard's Cafe on the other side. The parsonage was once a school, so it was a big two-story house with ten rooms and two bathrooms. We had two dining rooms, one for our family and the other was used for my dad and other ministers to have meetings. My dad was big on education, so we had a special room with a big table in it for reading and doing homework—there was his desk where he sat, to give us help if we had problems.

Reverend Simpkins and his family lived there before we did, and there was very little renovation done to convert the parsonage into living quarters. The walls were blackboards left over from the school, so my father painted over them, but as kids, we'd write on them anyway. At that time the church owned all the land behind it, which ran all the way to the creek, which is now the other side of Barksdale Boulevard. My dad enclosed the whole area with a fence, made swings out of old tires hanging from tree limbs, a play area for horseshoes, tennis and croquet, and on one side planted a big garden.

I had five brothers and one sister, and we all had chores to do everyday. After school my brothers would do the laundry because my mother would have the big pots already boiling on the open fire outside, one for cleaning, one for rinsing, and one for bluing. My sister washed the dishes and I would dry them. We all made our own beds. Dad did just about all of the cooking, and my sister Virginia would set the table and put the food on the table in big dishes, then call us in to eat. Each of us would say Bible verses and grace before every meal. After the chores, we'd go to the reading room for homework.

Whenever my parents would go out of town to another church, they'd get someone to stay with us, and Mrs. Leila Howard would feed us from her cafe because it was next door, and Dad would pay her when they returned. We had good parents. I can't remember a day that I'd come home and my mother wasn't there. All of my siblings and I played some sort of sports in school. As children and teenagers being raised in a parsonage, we had the best time together playing.

Other children would come to play with us in the backyard—sometimes it was like a schoolyard because there would be so many children. When the parents of the other children would come to pick them up, my dad would give them vegetables from his garden. As teenagers, we didn't go anywhere much because everybody would come to our house. The favorite game back then was horseshoes.

All seven of us went to college, and four of my five brothers went into the

Armed Services. When I was a teen, my dad bought a two-story house on East Valley Street with ten rooms. Shortly after he left the church, the parsonage was torn down, and a brick building was put up for the Parish House, which is still standing today next to the church.

—Interview by Beatrice Hill

Margaret Walker Santiago

Born in Charlotte, Margaret Walker Santiago moved to Spartanburg with her mother and two brothers, William and Lee Jr., in the mid-1930s. She attended Bethlehem Center kindergarten and Highland Elementary School. After third grade, her family moved to the "Baptistside" and became one of the first families in the newly-built Tobe Hartwell Apartments. After graduating from Carver High in 1948, she went to work at the Smithsonian Institute in Washington, D.C., where she retired as supervisor of the Natural History Museum Registrar.

My brother Lee Jr. had developed a kind of rheumatoid arthritis when he was in the eighth grade—that was before we moved to the project. We were on Beacon Street then. By the time we moved to the project, Lee could barely make it to school everyday, and my mother, being the sole provider of three children, had to work everyday. … My middle brother, William, had already missed two grades trying to take care of Lee while my mother worked.

When I was in the fifth grade, my brother William told my mother that I was big enough to start doing the dishes and helping around the house, so she then allowed me to start doing things, and helping to take care of Lee. It was then that I grew up. The project was right behind the school, so Mr. Harris [principal at Carrier Street Elementary] allowed me to go home two to three times a day to check on Lee, give him lunch and his medicine. The students at Carver High would bring his homework and take it back for him, and he passed his grade. This went on for two years until he died in 1942.

I remember the principal at Carver closed the school that day so the teachers and students could go to the funeral at Macedonia Church. I went to Cumming Street for the eighth grade and back to Carver until graduation. I recall Carver being a wonderful experience for me because I stayed busy all the time. I played basketball, was president of the pep club, all kinds of things. During that time, this story happened; I like to tell it because it had an impact on me and I think it had an impact on those involved.

That year I was chosen to be Miss Carver High—it was the first time that a tenth grader was chosen by a landslide. I had a coronation with all the works, and there were this group of girls that didn't like it [that I had been chosen]. Those girls got this slightly retarded girl to sneak up behind me and give me a hug (because she liked to hug everyone), and by her coming up behind, I didn't see her, and it startled me, so I turned around too quickly and hit her in the process, not intending to do so.

This same group of girls went to the Home Economics teacher and reported me as fighting, and that wasn't allowed if you were Miss Carver High. Anyway, they got together and held their little kangaroo court. There was a list of things that I was a member of, and they didn't want any of that, they wanted the title, so they took that and chose not to put my picture in the school annual as Miss Carver High. The next year I was chosen to be chairman of the girl's council.

My mother said no, so I got the principal to get her approval. Before I could accept that position, I had to write a speech about that experience of Miss Carver High. To show that I had rehabilitated myself, I had to go to every classroom and read that speech, and that is how I grew out of that experience. Now, I'm not proud that it happened, but I am glad that that kind of experience happened to me when I was very young. So now that I'm grown, I know how to handle situations.

There was a time when, as a child, you didn't have anyone to talk to but your mother, and she couldn't do anything about that because it was not in her authority to do so. If C.C. Woodson [principal of Carver] had not known his students like he did (and I think he knew every student that went through that school) a lot of students would have really gone the wrong way. He stood up for his students, if he knew you were doing the right thing or trying to do right.

The "Baptistside" was a great place when I lived down there. I recall one of my friends, Margaret Bomar, who lived back of the college [near Wofford], saying to me, "You know I used to think that all the people who live in the project were rich." [She said], "My father owned his own house, but when it rained, it rained on the beds, and in the winter, we had so much cover on us we couldn't turn over. I used to wish I could come live in the project."

I thought, what a change, from projects then to today, as to what they refer to as "the project." Just because you live in the project does not mean you're bad; because you don't have money like someone else, you don't have to be bad to come out of that situation. But society seems to think that living in one-parent households, or in a low-rent district, [brands you as] "those people," and that's kind of sad.

I didn't go up Liberty Street so much as a child, but the principal used to send me to take messages to the superintendent's office at Spartanburg High, with a token to ride the bus, but I'd walk up Liberty. I usually didn't pay much attention to what was there, but I remember Ellis's Cab stand, and Ms. Mamie Riley, who lived across the street from Ellis Cab, who had a cafe on the one block that black folk could go to downtown and have fun. That was Short Wofford, and those who were grown and liked the night life went there. Short Wofford was between Magnolia and Church Streets, not too far from the Carolina Theater. As a child I used to hear about Short Wofford and Ms. Mamie Riley's cafe. I couldn't wait until I got to the age where I could go there, because as a child you weren't allowed to go through there. I remember when I finally could go there, I went and I was shocked—it looked like a rat's den to me. There were these little huts that looked like little houses, and the owners would be just sitting there talking, and there were the shoeshine stands. It was nothing to be excited about, but Mamie Riley's name always comes up whenever people talk about Short Wofford.

Margaret Santiago lived in Washington, D.C., for many years while she worked for the Smithsonian Institution. When she retired, she moved to Luquillo, Puerto Rico, where she has lived for the past 14 years.

—Interview by Beatrice Hill and Brenda Lee

Kitty Collins Tullis

Kitty Collins, the oldest daughter of neighborhood entrepreneur Ernest L. Collins, grew up on East Park Avenue and South Liberty Street. A retired educator from the South Carolina School for the Deaf and the Blind, she is currently owner and operator of Collins Mortuary. Here she talks about the group of businesses her father owned on Liberty Street.

The Gulf station was on South Liberty Street next to the Church of the Epiphany— we lived next door to that. We first had the funeral home on Highland Avenue, and then my dad moved it to South Liberty Street, but it started on the upper end of Highland Avenue near West Main Street. On Liberty Street we had the service station and grocery store—more like the convenience store of today—the Blue Bird Cab, and the hotel. We called it the Liberty Street Hotel.

In the hotel, we had on the basement floor a cafe on one side, and the other side, we rented out to the Dr. Pepper Company, and they used that part to store crates and crates of drinks, and there is where the Dr. Pepper trucks would come and load up for delivery to different stores. The front side was the hotel, and on the side of that, facing Park Avenue, was the liquor store. My grandmother lived in the house behind the hotel on Park Avenue, and she had a beauty shop there.

Camp Croft came in, and at that time blacks didn't have any transportation, so my dad had the buses, and he would transport the black soldiers to and from Camp Croft. When that was over, he started the bus service for the black school system, because there were no buses for the black schools. He would take the football and basketball teams to play games at Duncan Park or other schools, and he wasn't paid by the district. This was one of his ways of giving back.

He had quite a few buses, and he started running a bus out in the county, to bring people to town on Saturdays. I think he charged maybe ten cents, and if you didn't have it, you'd get to ride anyway. That was how he was. When the buses broke down, he'd repair them at his own expense, because everybody was using them and paying almost nothing. He did this all on his own.

There were some nice houses on Liberty Street. Across the street from the funeral home was Mrs. Nina Wright's house; next to it was Dr. Mansel's office, and Mrs. McWhirter's home was next to that. On the same side of the funeral home was the Epiphany Church with the parsonage that used to be a school next to it, and next to that was Ms. Leila Howard's Cafe, then Booster Palmer's place where he had a newsstand-combination-beer-joint.

I remember "Schooner" Rogers' mother, Mrs. Robinson, was a seamstress, and they had a home down on Liberty. During those times, the housing project was a good place to live—it was nothing like what I'm hearing now about the projects. There was Dr. Bull who built a clinic there on Liberty, and next to it he built a drugstore for his nephew, Dr. Whaley. It was called Whaley's Pharmacy, and my uncle Joe Patton had a barbershop under the clinic. There was a place back then where all the teenagers used to hang out, down near the school, and it was run by Mr. Perry and his wife. My aunt Lillian Patton was raised by them; she was married to my uncle.

I think my daddy must have been a person with a vision back then, because he had buses when it wasn't thought of, and other things. When people talk about the single mother can't do this or that, I think about my grandmother who had my dad when she was only twelve years old. She was raped by her father in the cotton field, somewhere in the Wellford area. She moved here to Spartanburg and went to work for the Calhouns of Calhoun's Office Supply, who lived in Hampton Heights. They had a daughter that they named Kitty, and when she died, I was born, and they named me Kitty, and that is how I got my name, Kitty. My grandmother then started a restaurant, and brought her mother (my great-grandmother) and the rest of her family to Spartanburg from the Wellford area.

After leaving the Calhoun family, she bought an Esso service station; it was located on the corner of—which was unheard of then—Main Street and Highland Avenue. She ran it until the KKK came by with trouble, and she shot one of them. I don't think they bothered her much because of that, but she closed shortly after that. She did all of this on her own, a single mother, raised her son, sent him to a private high school, then sent him to college and he graduated. It was in that area that the funeral home started, before moving to Liberty Street.

The main places for black folk at that time were Short Wofford, Liberty Street; then there was Cumming Street, which was mostly residential in that area, but you always had professional people in parts of the black neighborhoods. When Camp Croft came in, they brought a lot of money to Spartanburg, and when they left, things just slowly went down.

—Interview by Beatrice Hill

Andrew Prysock

(courtesy, Raymond Floyd)

Andrew Prysock was born in Union County in 1919 and moved to Spartanburg with his parents, Will and Ella Prysock, when he was three years old. After returning from the armed services in World War II, he owned and operated Prysock's Shoe Repair on South Liberty Street. He later worked for and retired from Draper Corporation.

We lived on South Liberty Street, right where the C.C. Woodson Center is now. My family owned all of that property and sold it to the city to build the center. The city tried to place my parents in the Highland area [during urban renewal], but we fought against it, and they got the place across the street from the center, where they lived until they died.

I attended Carrier Street School and Cedar Hill Academy, which was a Baptist-supported school. When I quit school, I went to work at the Efird's department store [in downtown Spartanburg] in the shoe department. The manager there, who was W.O. Huntley, took me under his wing and taught me how to repair shoes. The more I did it the better I got, and before long I became the first black to manage a shoe repair on Main Street in downtown Spartanburg. After I passed the state board, I began to teach the handicapped [both black and white] students for the State of South Carolina how to repair shoes. I was making about twelve dollars per student. That was good money back then.

When I went into the Army, I was still into shoe repair of all types: regular, boots, orthopedic, etc. I taught shoe repair there. The fellows in the ROTC came out as second lieutenants, but my job was to teach the basic fundamentals of shoe repair, because they had shoe repair shops in the Army. When I came out of the Army, I started my own business on South Liberty

Street just below the Mount Moriah Baptist Church, and next to O'Shields Grocery Store. There was where I started teaching the students from Carver High School the basic fundamentals of shoe repair.

One day while I was teaching shoe repair, Professor Harris came in the shop, and I bragged about making good money. He looked at me (because he knew I had dropped out of school) and said, "Son, you are still going to need an education." In later years, I found that to be true. After about six years on Liberty Street, I went to work at the Draper Corp. for about 28 years, then I started another shop for shoe repair on Saint John Street and stayed there until urban renewal. I decided not to go anywhere else. I became the first black bailiff at the courthouse here in Spartanburg.

I remember growing up on the lower end of South Liberty Street. Back then we called that area Liberty Heights. It was at that time a cut above the rest in the black neighborhood, or so we thought. Most of the people that lived there owned their homes and property, and if anyone that was a bootlegger or hell raiser moved in the neighborhood, they'd get run off. As teens and young adults we'd always go up on the "Baptistside" and do our partying and raising the ruckus, then we'd come back to the Heights as angels. We used to refer to the other part of Liberty, Cudd, and the Cemetery Street area as the "Baptistside." This is before the Tobe Hartwell Projects were built in 1941.

As a child I worked for Mrs. Leila Howard because she lived up the street from my family in Liberty Heights, just around the corner from [where] Dr. Bull built his house. She raised cows, so my job was to help feed the cows, take the wagon and bring her milk to her, all before I went to school. One morning I forgot to brush all the hay off my clothes and the teacher whipped me because she thought I'd been fooling around before school. That is when my father took me out of Carrier Street and sent me to Cedar Hill. After school I would take Mrs. Leila's cows out to pasture, down to the field in the back of what is now Phyllis Goins. Everyday she'd pay me ten or fifteen cents. This was big money for me because I was only about nine or ten years old.

Liberty Street was where all the black business was—shoe repair, funeral homes, ice house, filling station, you name it and it was there. There were some nice homes scattered here and there, but a lot of them were shack-looking houses. It was those shack-looking houses that held the parties. Most of the time the up-to-do or sporty class of people gave these parties. We would call them the ten-cent shimmy party, and all it was was a group of people that charged you ten cents to come in and dance all night if you wanted to.

The party was usually held at a person's house who couldn't pay the rent for that week, and these parties were held all over town in the black neighborhoods. They were called ten-cent shimmies because the cover charge was ten-cent, but it was really a rent party to help someone pay their rent. Back then, house rent was only about a $1.50 or $2.00 a week. In the Cemetery Street area sometimes the house would only have about two rooms, and some places the houses would be so raggedy, the landlord only charged 50 or 75 cents.

The landlord was too glad to have anybody in those houses because an empty house in those neighborhoods meant firewood to the neighbors, plank by plank, especially in the winter.

Urban renewal was good because it took people out of the slum areas. Integration was good for a lot of people, but I've never had any problems before or after.

—Interview by Beatrice Hill

Dr. John W. Coleman

John Coleman was born in Spartanburg in 1920 and attended Carrier Street School. He graduated from Cumming Street School in 1937, where he was salutatorian of the class. While waiting on an acceptance letter from medical school, Coleman and his best friend, Royal Sims, opened the popular Blue Lantern Club on South Liberty Street in the early 1940s. Coleman left Spartanburg to go to medical school, where he became a radiologist, but the Blue Lantern continued, closing in the early 1960s. Dr. Coleman died January 1, 2005.

In 1941 when I graduated from Johnson C. Smith University, I came home to Spartanburg to work with my father. I had a good friend [Royal] who lived there in Spartanburg, and he was working at the Spartanburg Laundry. He and I have been good buddies all through high school. I remember he had to quit school to take care of his sister's children. He and I decided to open up a cafe.

There was this place on the corner of South Liberty Street and Hampton Avenue. I think it was 428 South Liberty Street, right across from the Majority Baptist Church. We rented the place, and we didn't have a cook, so I had an uncle who cooked for the road construction people, and since we were just coming out of the Depression, he wasn't working at that time. We thought it would be nice if we asked him to come and run the place, and he said yes, he would be glad to.

We opened the cafe and we didn't have a name for it. When I was in college, I went to Greensboro and there was a cafe there called the Red Lantern, so I thought, why don't we call ours the Blue Lantern? We had blue lanterns inside the place and blue lanterns in the windows, blue tablecloths, the whole motif was blue. This was late 1941, and the place did very well. There was an Army Base in Camp Croft, and they had recruits from the war who would come often, and the place did well because of that.

We tried to have a first-class place, so we had a license to sell beer and wine but not liquor. We didn't want to sell liquor because the place was right across the street from Majority Church, and we thought it wouldn't be right. We didn't sell wine either. We could have but at that time people thought if you sold wine that you would be serving liquor also, so we decided to just sell beer, and that place did well.

Things began to happen. I got a draft notice from the Army, and I had already been accepted into medical school in Tennessee. So I took the draft notice to the draft board along with my papers, showing I was accepted in medical school, and I showed them both to the one in charge there, who happened to be a white physician. He looked at them both, and tore up my draft notice, and told me to go on to medical school, but check in with him when I came home on break to let him know I was doing all right, and I did that.

In September 1942, I had to leave for medical school, [and] Royal and my uncle stayed to run the Blue Lantern. About six or eight months after I left, Royal got drafted into the Army, so he sold his share to my uncle, and my parents took care of my part. Between them, they kept the place going for about five years. When my parents found out that I was not coming back to Spartanburg after graduating from medical school, they sold my part to my uncle and he ran it for a few years; after that I don't know what happened to it. I didn't come back home to practice because I was advised by other physicians that Spartanburg didn't offer the opportunities for black doctors of my specialty, which is radiology.

—Interview by Beatrice Hill and Brenda Lee

Willie B. Wilson Jr.

(courtesy, Raymond Floyd)

Willie B. Wilson was born in the Cemetery Street area on December 1, 1922, to Maude and Willie B. Wilson Sr. A World War II veteran, he worked as a dry cleaner-presser before going to work as a stock clerk at Aug. W. Smith, where he retired after many years of service. He is the father of Beatrice Hill.

There were four of us siblings then, and years later a fifth one was adopted. We lived on a little short street that was just off Cemetery Street, called "Dog Hollow." It was not paved, so it was muddy when it rained. This was in the mid- to late-'20s, so at that time none of the houses had running water nor electric lights. We used kerosene lamps for lights, and in the winter the fireplace added more light.

There were two spigots outside, one on each end of the street, and everybody got their water from there. The bathrooms were outhouses, with about three for every six or eight houses. These houses were merely shacks, just pieces of wood thrown together. In the winter, we would make a paste of flour and water to seal the cracks in the walls and floors, trying to keep the cold air out. A lot of people were very poor back then, but they survived. By the mid-'50s most of those houses had a fresh coat of paint, electric lights, running water, and bathrooms were put on the back porch, but [they were] were the same houses nonetheless. Those were the only houses that urban renewal should have targeted.

I started school at Carrier Street to the seventh grade. By that time Cedar Hill Academy was gone, and they had started to build Carver High, but we went to Cumming Street School for the eighth grade, then to Carver in 1939. Some of the students stayed on at Cumming until graduation. Back then you graduated from the eleventh grade.

As a youngster, I worked at the local grocery store, delivering groceries. At that time you could buy almost anything for a nickel—sugar, flour, bacon, just about anything you wanted for five cents. Some people had telephones, and they would call in their orders. If it was two dollars' worth of groceries, I would have to make two trips to deliver them. There was a cleaner by the name of H. B. on the corner of Dunbar and Main where I started sweeping floors, and eventually learned how to press clothes.

In 1943 I went into the Army. At that time the Army was segregated. We had a few fighting outfits, but most of the black soldiers were in the service outfits—we called it Quartermaster. We were in charge of all the supplies that the soldiers on the front lines would need—clothing, food, medicine. Anything the soldiers needed, my outfit had it. We were the Service Battalion. Most of the soldiers were sent out of state for training. Very few from South Carolina were trained in Camp Croft. I was trained in Mississippi before being shipped off to France.

I remember before World War II, there were hardly any jobs, and the poor people had to get commodities from the Armory on North Liberty Street. It was similar to the food stamp program of today. The government would send out a paper to the families to come and get food on certain days. We used to call it black flour, but it was brown in color with black specks. Butter, powdered milk were all government-issued. The people that did have jobs got paid very little, and even they had certain days to buy different foods because the Armed Services had to get their food first. I remember when ladies couldn't buy silk stockings on certain days, because the Army used silk for the parachutes.

That was so long ago, but that was the time when you could buy ice for your ice box from the ice man, who would come through our neighborhood on Sunday mornings with a wooden wagon driven by a horse. Sometimes he'd let me ride with him and hold the reins and we'd deliver ice all over town. You could buy a five-, ten- or twenty-five cent block. We had an ice house on Liberty Street next to Cromer's Store, and on the other side Mr. Jim Young owned a cleaner, but he let somebody else run it, and there was another cleaner down from there run by Mr. Gillam.

I ate dinner at Mrs. Leila Howard's place all the time. She had good food.

She had a nice clean place, and anybody could go in there, as long as you behaved. She looked a lot like Mary McLeod Bethune, and she smoked cigars, but she was a real nice person. There was the parsonage and the Church of the Epiphany next to her place. Reverend Brown and his family lived in the parsonage. About two or three times a year they would have a big party with all kinds of different colored flags hanging around the yard. You could go and have a good time.

We usually had our fun going to the ten-cent shimmy rent parties. There were two brothers, Willie and Walt Fuller—they could really play the heck out of a piano—and that was our music, they could play anything. Most of the time wherever the party was, there was a piano, and the Fuller brothers would be there.

There were the cab companies, Ellis and Carver cabs, right there on Liberty Street. We had an eighteen-hole golf course over next to Cemetery Hill. Mrs. Nina Coln's brother, A.C. Coln, had it fixed up real nice—this was before Duncan Street started building up and before Tobe Hartwell was built, in the mid to late '30s.

There was also a small putt-putt golf course behind Collins Funeral Parlor, and another one next to Lewis Hanes' place—it later became the Southside Cafe. The area from Main Street to Arkwright was called the Southside, and the area between Park Avenue and Clement Street was called the "Baptistside," and the area between East Valley and Cemetery Streets was called the "Red Light district" because that is where all the happenings were—the gambling, whiskey—and the police always patrolled that area to keep folks from killing each other. Once you passed that area, things cooled down.

On Friday nights the soldiers came to town, and they would be everywhere, all over the place. At that particular time, if you lived on Park Avenue you were considered as being in the upper class, but if you lived on certain parts of Cemetery, or in an alley, you were considered as low-class people, where there was always trouble. Mrs. Liza had a cafe there, and there was "Hurry" George, as we called him—he had an ice cream parlor. There was the pool room, and Dawkins-Smith was first a shoeshine parlor run by Mrs. Fannie Young's son, Joe.

The USO was down from Carrier Street, and farther down was Liberty

Heights. I remember Mr. Shavers had his place next to Mrs. Howard's cafe, and he had the big, juicy, good hamburgers, the best in town. There were times when the circus came to town, and sometimes it would be on the school ground below Carrier Street School (this is before Carver was built), and sometimes it would be in the vacant lot just off Cemetery Street. This was the famous minister Earle Lee Backus [who] had a circus. They had a band that would march from the site up to Main Street and back again. Back when it was cold, the tent was heated by wood fires in the big 50-gallon drums, and he had white and black audiences. The white people would sit in the middle aisles and the blacks would sit on bleachers around the wall. There were rides and games that only cost about ten cents. That was a lot of money, because people didn't make much money back then. Times were hard then, but we got through.

—Interview by Beatrice Hill

Ira Tucker

Gospel songwriter and lead singer of the Dixie Hummingbirds, Ira Tucker was born May 17, 1925, on Golden Street in the Gas Bottom area of Spartanburg. Perhaps the most successful black gospel group of all time, the Hummingbirds were featured in a 1995 documentary, "We Love You Like a Rock," and the book "Great God A'Mighty: The Dixie Hummingbirds and the Rise of Soul Gospel Music" (2003) by Jerry Zolten. In this June 2004 telephone interview, Tucker, 81, shared his memories of his childhood in Spartanburg.

There was Layton's bicycle shop [on South Liberty Street] where we used to go to get our bicycles repaired if something would happen to them. That must have been around 1938 or '39, maybe a bit further back, '36 or '37. I was a grocery boy, riding groceries for Jones Food Store. I remember way down South Liberty, they had—well, it wasn't on Liberty Street— they had that one-day church down there, that church they built in one day. I delivered everywhere from Hampton Heights, all the way down Pine Street, and down to Liberty Street—my grocery route was all down through there.

My mother was born in Newberry. My mother used to get [news]papers down there in the country; people would put in help-wanted ads. She looked in the want ads and saw Mr. Jim Burnett in Spartanburg, S.C., so she wrote him, and they said OK come on, so that's how she got to Spartanburg. I wasn't even born then, but my mother was pregnant. Mr. Burnett made a basket to go under the gas stove in the kitchen, and my mother would put me under there, to keep me warm. I was living on a little street called Golden Street right across from the house, 175 Golden Street. That's how that was.

I used to go by South Liberty Street. Sometime I would take groceries there. During that time, black people were only limited to certain places to go. I furnished a lot of stores and the people who ran the restaurants. I started riding that bike and people would stop their cars and laugh at me [because] I was so small and I could just barely touch the pedals. People would say, "How can he carry a great big crate of groceries like that as small as he is?" They would get so tickled. When I started I wasn't but nine years old.

I worked for Allman & Bridges. They were on Saint John. I worked for Adair and Little. They were on East Main. And I worked for Jones Food Store. The first job I had I worked for a butcher man, Mr. Turner on Saint John, $1 per week! Today I can make any kind of sausage that you could eat. That man taught me. He didn't pay me much, but he taught me a lot!

There were three boys in my family, Johnny, Eugene and Ira. They are both gone. I was the middle boy. My mother was Maggie. My grandfather was Ed Moore. My mother was Maggie Moore before she married. It was rough coming up. I just felt like I could make it. I've always had a feeling that regardless of what it is, I can get over it.

Short Wofford was the black Main Street. There was a guy called Blind Simmie [Dooley]. He used to play a guitar, blues and all, and people would give him money, nickels and dimes and all. I was a kid but I heard him.

I knew [R&B singer] Arthur Prysock. He worked at the Spartanburg Shoe Hospital. Arthur had an uncle named Isaiah Porter. He was a piano player. Then his brother Red Prysock, he was right there. Then they went to Greensboro. They stayed there for years, too, but their native home was in Spartanburg.

There was a guy called Trottin' Sally. I have seen him in person. When I was a kid, he would come and talk to my grandfather. He never wore any shoes. I knew him but I was afraid of him. He was marked by a horse. He could be talking to you and [then] "hee-hee-hee-ah-ah-ah" like a horse. And run, he could outrun the cars of that day, yes! We were living back over on Golden Street then, off of Crawford Avenue. There was a big place called the Hall House. That's where we were living. And Trottin' Sally would come by there, and that man had a violin and honest to God, he'd say, "Good morning," and that thing would say, "Good morning." I never heard a man play an instrument like that. I must have been 5 or 6. A lot of people were afraid of him, but he didn't bother anybody. I haven't heard anybody play a violin like that today! He could make the thing almost talk. And where did he get it from?

I met Blind Simmie and I met Bus Porter. I got a tape on Bus Porter and all of the old singers that were around there in Spartanburg. Bus was grown when I was a kid. I used to say I wish I could sing like him.

There was a guy down there—he had a dog called Buster the Wonder Dog. He could do things you wouldn't believe. He traveled around with that dog. He'd lay down ten cigarettes, and he'd say, "You go get the Camel out of there." And he'd go get the Camel. And he'd say, "If you got hit by a car, how would you be?" And he'd just lay down. He performed everywhere. He'd just walk the streets. He'd say, "Want to see him do a few tricks?" and people'd say, yeah. That's how he got his audience. He'd be around close to every store where people were, you know. And people would applaud for him. He'd say, "How do you walk when your leg's hurting?" and he'd be hopping. I don't know how he taught that dog all that. Buster the Wonder Dog. [He'd ask] who had the biggest feet in the crowd—that dog could find them. He'd go to their shoes. He was great.

I had a group called the Royal Lights before I got with the Dixie Hummingbirds. We sang at Golden Street Church. We sang down at the church … wherever we could sing, wherever they wanted us. The House of Prayer. That was west, that's where I joined the Hummingbirds after going to hear them there one night.

The Hummingbirds had been singing way before I joined [them]. When they would come to town, there was a big tree right there by the Golden Street Baptist Church and I used to climb that tree and look in the church and listen to them. They didn't have mics then but you could hear them. I said, "Oh, I wish one day I could travel and sing like that!" And I said well, I'm going to see if I can make a start. I've always been aggressive, trying to do things that people said you couldn't do. They didn't think I was going to be able to sing anything but what I was singing. I was a baritone. I told the fellows, "Look Mr. [James] Davis, if I can't sing the tenor, I'm only 29 miles from Spartanburg and I'll walk back home. You don't have to take me back. If I can't do it, I'll walk back home." Sixty-five years I've been with them.

I left Spartanburg when I was 14 with the same group that I'm with now.

Ira Tucker, now 80 years old, lives in Philadelphia with his wife, Louise. He continues to sing with the Dixie Hummingbirds.

—Interview by Betsy Teter

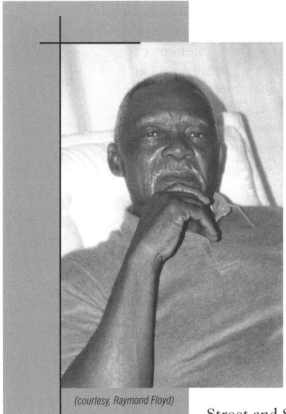
(courtesy, Raymond Floyd)

Dewey Tullis

Dewey Tullis, born in 1927, grew up in Miami and met his wife, Spartanburg's Kitty Collins, when they attended West Virginia State College together. Here he describes the neighborhood he came to in the 1950s. For many years he was a teacher and administrator in the Greenville County School system. Now retired, he is director of funerals for Collins Mortuary.

I came to Spartanburg during the summer of 1950. Not having any money, I rode the bus up here, and [the Collins family] picked me up from the station and brought me to their filling station. You see, at the intersection of East Lee Street and South Liberty Street is where the segregated part of Spartanburg began. Once you were across Lee Street it was almost the feeling that Br'er Rabbit had in the briar patch—free at last. Because Liberty Street was a beautiful thing! What I mean by that is, you see, everybody spoke to each other: "Hey, how you doing?" or "Come here, child, let me tell you something," that sort of thing. It was a spirit of comradery, friendly. The people were friendly.

Businesses were on the left side going down toward Caulder Avenue. On the right side, of course, we had the alleys and places like that, but on the front part of the street were some very nice, almost expensive homes. There were Dr. Douglas, the Grays, the Chestnuts down by the school, and then further up you had the Youngs, McWhirters, Mansels, the Deans, and more nice, family homes. At that time a man could get off work on Friday, cash his check there on Liberty Street, and pick up his laundry, because there were two ladies that did laundry for people right there in the neighborhood. There were cafes all around so you didn't have to go far to get something to eat, then you could get groceries down the street on the corner at the store. We had just about everything on that street. On the corner on Park and Liberty Street my father-in-law, E. L. Collins, had a hotel. There was a building there, you see, being the type of man he was, when the black soldiers of Camp Croft would come to town on Saturday night they would have a place to stay, and of course the liquor store was there in the hotel, and they could buy their liquor right there.

E. L. Collins was an entrepreneur. Let me tell you something: at that time in Spartanburg that street was already alive, and whenever people went away on vacation or away to school, [and] when they came home, they would come down Liberty Street. It was THE place to go. I believe that at that time Liberty Street was equivalent to the famous Beale Street [in Memphis], or the famous 125th Street [in New York].

On those streets there was a spirit, a kind of good feeling in the air. Looking back, I wish we had thought about creating a Liberty Street with that kind of feeling. One of these days somebody ought to write a book about it—about how we were looking for something that we already had. We had a sense of togetherness, and a sense of helping each other and that sort of thing. People looked out for each other.

You would have to understand that … you didn't have a policeman on every corner, you did not have policemen patrolling the area—we policed our own area. We knew who was bad or who was likely to start trouble, and most of the time one of us could talk to those people to calm them down. During those times you could leave your door open and not worry about it. If a child got in the street, somebody would get the child and say "come 'ere chile, you stay with me 'til yo' folks come" and later the family would come for their child and say, "Thank you." That was all.

Togetherness in the Liberty Street area was a beautiful experience of people living together. It had the businesses, and of course your poor homes; it also had some of the best homes in the black community on it. As you go down on the left side and you turn to go to the cemetery, there was the infamous Cemetery Street. It was down in there that you had the old shack houses that we lived in when we came out of slavery. Those old houses were in every southern city. All you had to do when you visited a town was to find the railroad tracks and there nearby was the black community with those old shotgun houses.

—Interview by Beatrice Hill and Brenda Lee

Fannie Richie and her daughter, Traci, in 1968

Fannie Richie

Fannie Richie, born in 1942, moved to the Southside in the sixth grade and was a 1960 graduate of Carver High School. She is retired from Pet Dairy and now enjoys working in her church and community.

I lived in the Highland community until I was about twelve years old, and the rest of my history is on the Southside. I cried when I left Highland, and I cried when I had to leave South Liberty Street [during urban renewal]. We lived at 178 Rigby Avenue, which ran from South Liberty to South Converse Street. Now, the creek at the bottom of the hill separated the black from the white folk. The part we (black folk) lived on was not paved—it was a dirt road—but across the creek, going into South Converse was paved because that is where the white people lived.

Next door to us was a house facing Liberty Street. It was from that point going up toward town, that [began the] homes of white people, and from that point going down toward Caulder Avenue were all black folk. When we moved in on Rigby, the white family next door to us moved, and we moved into their house on South Liberty where we stayed a long time. When we heard that the Model Cities was coming through there, and they were placing people in different places, we went ahead and started looking ourselves, and found this place, because we didn't want to be put in a place we didn't like.

I grew up on South Liberty Street in the fifties. When we first moved there it came in just right, because I was twelve and going to the seventh grade at Carver, so I could walk to school down the street. The first friend I met, who is now deceased, was Beulah Petty. She, Frances Wellman, and Barbara Smith all lived close to me, only a few houses apart. We all walked to school, studied, and played together. During the summer while school was out, most of the kids would work picking peaches or beans to make money to buy their clothes for the next school term, or some would go out of town visiting relatives.

Going down Liberty Street, you had everything. Most of the teenagers would come from the north side, or the Highland area. They came because this is where everything was—you had the school with all of its activities, like football and basketball games, and the center that was once the USO for the soldiers. At one time the soldiers from Donaldson Air Force Base would come and have their dances there. There was the Southside Cafe with Mrs. Abercrombie who sold sandwiches, sodas, and ice cream, and there was Whaley's Pharmacy, later called Oliver's Pharmacy—those were hangouts for teens.

Across the street from our house, there was the Buccaneer Club with the Masonic Lodge upstairs, barbershop downstairs in the back, and Deluxe Cab in the adjoining lot. There was Bull's clinic where you had a dentist, a doctor's office, and, in the basement, there was another barbershop and living quarters where Dr. Whaley had his apartment, which later became Young's photography studio. Next door to the clinic was Gadsden [Photo] Studio and North Carolina Mutual Insurance, and next was the drugstore.

Going down the street on the corner was Ernest Collins and his businesses: the hotel, liquor store, full-service gas station, grocery store, bail bonding and funeral home, plus he owned other rental properties elsewhere.

He also owned the only bus line we (black folk) had at one time. He would use the buses to take the school kids on trips. The football and basketball teams would also use it, and the churches used it for their picnics. This was one man I have always admired because he was independent and always doing things to help his people. There was Dr. Mansel, who would make house calls. We had a lot of professionals, and you had your regular people. This was the Southside, where we had everything and it was enough—before Model Cities came through and wiped it out, just took away our history.

There was a lady we called Ma Blanche, who was the mother of E. L. Collins, who operated a club called the Victory Tavern. You had to be 21 to go there, and we couldn't wait to get grown so we could go there. It was a fact that young people did not socialize with the grownups. They had certain places for the professionals like teachers and business people to go and socialize, and you had separate places for the young folk. The only places we saw the teachers were at school or if they had a need to talk to your parents. You just didn't mingle with the grownups. Now everybody is mingling together.

—Interview by Beatrice Hill and Brenda Lee

James "Patch" Talley

James Talley was born in the Cemetery Street area on the Southside and grew up in Phyllis Goins Court. In 1959 he graduated from Carver High School, then had a long career as a teacher and coach. In 1993 he became the first black mayor of the city of Spartanburg.

My remembrance of South Liberty Street is there were about 50 or more black businesses up and down Liberty Street, and they answered the need of the community, mostly the black community. They had just about everything that we needed, from grocery stores to dry cleaners, movies, shoeshine parlors, poolroom, restaurants, you name it, it was there.

Now Liberty Street wasn't big on retail, which was in the downtown area. On the south side of town there was a new life for most people, predominately blacks. Most of the time there was harmony— you had people that knew each other, a neighbor that was concerned about a neighbor. You had a child that couldn't go too wrong, because everybody was a father or a mother to the children in that community. If you stepped out of line, your mother and father would know about it, and if you did something good, they would still know about it.

The clinic, barbershops, doctors' offices, mortuaries and the Masonic lodge [were all there]. There also was a social aspect there, so the Southside was a microcosm of a city, and in that city I think the people had a really full life. Some of my most memorable moments of that time were at Carver High School because that was the center of everything that happened in the community. Another memory was the recreation center, called the USO, [which] was within walking distance at maybe two hundred yards from the school. Whatever happened at the school, it continued at the USO.

There was a social aspect there: plays, dances, social functions, and things like that for the kids happened right there at the school and the USO. The thing I remember most … would be the fact that the teachers at Carver were not just at the school, they were throughout the community. No matter what you did, you could almost always run into a teacher or a minister, because they were all over the community, so as a child you had to be on guard with your behavior everywhere. Your parents knew all of these people, so you had to be just like you were at home in front of them.

What I'm really saying is, the family aspect, the family feeling that you had: as you were not a stranger in that neighborhood, which was from Jenkins Junior High to Arkwright. Everybody knew you, they knew whose child you were, so if anything went wrong, it was found out at home. When I think of happy moments, of course I think of playing, the spray pool in the old projects (Tobe Hartwell), I think of skating down the big hill on Young Street.

There was a curve near the Sanctified Church where Mrs. Jeanette Jones would beat the piano and sing. She lived next to the church, and sometimes we'd walk by her house just to hear her singing and playing the piano there on Young Street. Then you'd think of Martins Alley, Clement, and Cudd Streets. It's such a broad memory, it's almost impossible to bring it down to one particular spot. When I think about it, I see this mural of things that happened on the Southside. I'd see myself walking down Liberty Street, passing each business there. It was a wonderful era.

—Interview by Beatrice Hill and Brenda Lee

Frank Nichols Jr.

(courtesy, Raymond Floyd)

A member of the fourth generation of a family that came to Spartanburg in the 1800s, Frank Nichols Jr. was born in 1942 and reared in the family home on Cudd Street. Frank was a brick and tile mason and later retired from the city of Spartanburg in communications.

The area where we lived was quiet because there were a lot of older people in that section, and there was not a lot of noise. There were houses that had kids around my age, but for the most part, it was peaceful. I remember Reverend Earle, who was an old man that lived down a few houses from us, and whenever he would be driving down the street, we sat on his bumper and would ride, because he drove so slow. That was fun.

Across the street from our house was just a big open field, with a branch running through it. On the other side of the branch were the backyards of white families that lived on Ridgewood Avenue. Everything was segregated at that time, but as kids, we played together in that open field without any conflict. I remember David West, whose mother was a nurse. They had a big backyard, so we played there a lot. There was Farmer [Cliff] Gray's two sons, Dustin and his brother, who played with us. We'd have the best times together.

In my family, I was the oldest of four: two sisters, Ann, and Marilyn, and one brother, Dallas. I started kindergarten on South Liberty Street next to the Episcopal Church and then went to Carrier Street for first grade. We went to Highland school while waiting for Mary H. Wright to be completed. In seventh grade we went to Carver High, and sometimes after school we'd go to Duncan Park to play ball on the little league field. I remember the

Spartanburg Peaches team playing on the big field, and we'd go behind the fence to search for balls that were knocked over. One of the balls I had from their last game, with their autographs, I kept for a long time until my brother lost it outside playing with it.

By the time I got to high school I was playing in all of the sports. After graduation in 1960, I worked with O. B. Gray in ceramic tile for a while, then I went into the Army and was a security agent. I remember on Liberty Street there was the Bull's Clinic, Oliver's Pharmacy, the Blue Lantern, Majority Baptist Church, the Episcopal kindergarten, and Ernest Collins, who had the chartered bus service that took our teams to and from different schools to play football and basketball games.

In that same area was Ellis Cafe, and there was the Southside Cafe run by Mrs. Nancy Abercrombie. It was there where the teams would go after the games and eat. During that time there were several black businesses in the area where you could go and eat. Most of the guys during that era dressed a bit better than the young men do now. … There were shoeshine parlors everywhere, so our shoes looked good, and some of us would shop at the men's stores, like Price's, Greenewald's, Gilbert and Son's. Those stores had real nice and some expensive clothing. We didn't have a lot of money, but we worked odd jobs just to buy one or two pieces so we could dress nice and neat.

Our school principal, Mr. Woodson, ran a tight ship. Respect was top priority. Even your neighbors could discipline you. We didn't have a lot of things back then, but we respected our parents, our teachers, and all grownups. I remember when I graduated from high school, there wasn't a college in Spartanburg that a black student could go to, and now you have six, including Sherman. There were several kids that I went to school with who were smart kids but couldn't go out of town to college because they had to work and help out at home with other siblings. Had it not been for segregation, they could have stayed here, worked and gone to college.

Through the years when I went to school at Carver High, I had always heard of the schools being separate but equal. We lived closer to Spartan High, but it was the time of segregation, so no matter how close you lived to a white school, you had to walk or ride the bus to a black school. The YMCA was part of Spartan High's curriculum, where they'd go for swim lessons.

They also had a gym and auditorium, among other things that we didn't have. At Carver High, we only had a gym that doubled for an auditorium, no swim lessons for black kids at the YMCA. Things were separate but not equal.

—Interview by Beatrice Hill

(courtesy, Raymond Floyd)

Wilhelmina Hollis

Wilhelmina Hollis was born on Cemetery Alley March 27, 1946, and later moved to Tobe Hartwell Apartments. The stay-at-home mom fondly remembers the times when her neighborhood was like a village.

I was raised in the house with my grandmother and my mother, Janie Gault Fowler. We lived in Cemetery Alley, where any adult could chastise you. Some of the people I remember very well: there was Bob Beatty, who sang with a quartet; Mrs. Lucille Young; Bobby Young and all his siblings, who were like big sisters and big brothers to me, and others.

There was old man Charlie Murphy, who had a horse-drawn wooden wagon. On Halloween he would take us on hay rides. He was just like everybody's grandpa. The creek down by "Dog Hollow" was where we went to catch tadpoles, before Tobe Hartwell Extension was built. We'd help Mrs. Emma Hipps with milking her cow, and there was a billy goat behind the kindergarten, and we'd tease him and run. Most of the older people had a flower garden of some sort, and we'd help them weed their gardens, and there was Mrs. Jo Ella, who would always keep our balls when they rolled in her yard.

My memories are many when I think of the old neighborhood because we enjoyed ourselves—we had fun. Our neighbors were like our parents. I don't think there was anybody that grew up in the Cemetery Street area who didn't know Charles "Pap" Talley. He was the neighborhood father, uncle, big brother to all the children, just an all-around super nice person that everyone loved and respected. When it came to discipline, he had a very big impact on my life, [giving me] advice that has helped me through the years.

A carnival would come to Spartanburg every year over on Cemetery Street, and the older kids in the neighborhood, would take the smaller kids. I remember Mr. Wofford's dog, named Bebo, and wherever you went, you'd have to pass and out run the dog, to get from one place to another. I remember taking baths in the big tin tub, helping Grandma wash clothes in the big black wash pots over the fire, and the bluing for the white clothes. There were about three families to one outhouse, no inside toilets, no electricity. We used kerosene lamps.

Financially we were poor, but we were rich because we had so much love, respect, that we shared with each other that extended through the neighborhood. There was no such thing as, "You can't make my children mind." Our neighbors were our parents. If your parents had to work, the neighbors watched you, and when they ate, you ate. Almost all of the houses in the alley had beds in all of the rooms except the kitchen. My granddad always kept plenty of wood and coal on hand for the winter months.

When we moved to the housing project, I felt like I had died and gone to heaven. I didn't realize how much we didn't have until we moved. We had an inside bathroom, running water, electricity, hot water, all inside the house. I think I took three or four baths in one day when we first moved into the projects. Remembering the old neighborhood, I think about Cromer's store and how the old people would send a note or call, and James Dogan would deliver their groceries. They didn't have to worry about getting out to the store.

Back then [there] was no such thing as going on vacation because we couldn't afford it, but the local churches always had their annual picnics in Shelby, North Carolina, at Holly Oak Park, which was a popular resort for blacks back then. Everyone that wanted to go could go for free. Some would go in cars or ride the church bus—that was as close to a vacation as we got. I wish that my children could have experienced some of the things I went through as a child, because it was those things that made me strong and [taught me] how to appreciate things.

—Interview by Beatrice Hill

George Foster

George Foster, born in 1943 on Cudd Street, was a junior and a member of the youth chapter of the NAACP at Carver High School in 1960 when plans were made to conduct a "sit-in" at the lunch counter of Woolworth's in downtown Spartanburg. Here he relates the story of what happened that day.

Staying active in sports was what I liked to do, so I played baseball, football, and basketball. Somehow the principal got word about the plans for a sit-in and he told the coaches to talk to me. Well, they told me I only had one year to go and I shouldn't get involved because I could get put out of school.

I participated in marches and sit-ins in different places, and [in] Columbia, South Carolina. I was working with the NAACP people, and we had a meeting with other officials of the NAACP over on Dean Street the night before, and the sit-in was scheduled that night to take place the next day. [It so] happened that after the meeting was over, a decision was made to cancel it, but no one called me or my buddy,

Big Boy Campbell, to tell us the sit-in was not taking place.

The next day Big Boy and I went uptown to Woolworth's on Main Street in Spartanburg. We waited for the others to show, not knowing they weren't coming. After a while of waiting outside the store, we decided to go in. It was going to be a big sit-in with more people, but it was only the two of us there. So, we go in and sit down at the lunch counter and asked for a menu. The people behind the counter just sort of looked at us and walked away. Nothing happened.

We sat there for a while, and soon there was no one sitting there but us. In a few minutes there were these two big white men coming through the door toward us like they were going to kill us, so we stood up, and after a few words between them and us, someone called the police. We were arrested and they took us to jail. I don't think we stayed in jail overnight, just a few hours. I believe the attorney's name was Matthew Perry because he was in court with us, and after he pleaded our cases the judge charged us anyway and let us go.

I didn't feel any pressure, nor was I afraid to do this, because it always bothered me when I saw the "white only" signs. I don't know whether it bothered me more than most people, but it bothered me. I think what led me to this point was, in my junior year in high school, we had the championship [football] game and we won. The Spartanburg *Herald* newspaper gave us about a two-inch article. Spartan High also had a game the same night, and they had a tied game, but the Spartanburg *Herald-Journal* gave them practically a whole page. They always thought Spartan High was better than us.

Shortly after that, I wrote a letter to the newspaper challenging Spartan High to play us around Thanksgiving for a benefit game to help feed the needy people, and they printed the letter in the paper. I remember Ms. Louvenia Barksdale talking to me about it because it was a good idea. I think after that, all of the surrounding black high schools started doing it. It's always been with me—the segregation—how it hurts. I remember [at] the marches in Columbia, we had to promise not to retaliate during the marches. We were supposed to endure all of the violence but stand firm. People there were shouting all kinds of obscenities and spitting on us as we walked by, and we were arrested.

The people thought that because you were black you were not as good a person as the white person. All of this was on my mind in junior high school. It bothered me, so I was willing to do something about it. I didn't think about the consequences or that I might have been killed or something, I just knew that segregation was not right and I wanted to make it right. I think the people in Woolworth's were more shocked than I was, because this had never happened in Spartanburg before, although it was happening elsewhere, even as close as Greenville with Jesse Jackson.

I remember when this was happening, my grandmother, whom I lived with then, was working for this rich white family (I don't remember their names), and I think they threatened my grandmother with the loss of her job. I asked her, and she said that the family spoke to her about it. They also spoke to Mr. [Principal C.C.] Woodson because I was a student there at Carver. What's so ironic about it was, years later, my sister was working in this nursing home for the elderly, and there was this lady from the rich family, she was old and didn't know she was in the world, and my sister had to take care of her.

The KKK burned a cross in Mr. Smith's yard, which was right across the street from me, right there on Caulder Avenue. I guess they got the houses mixed up. There weren't too many people from the Spartanburg area involved in the marches and sit-ins at that time, and you couldn't really blame them, because it was no picnic to have people spitting on you and you couldn't do anything about it.

Now living in New York, Foster is retired from the Administrative Office of Labor Relations and Collective Bargaining for the city of New York school system.

—Interview by Beatrice Hill

Donald W. Beatty

(courtesy, Raymond Floyd)

Don Beatty grew up in Tobe Hartwell during the 1950s and '60s and was part of a big family. He graduated in 1970 with the last class to graduate from Carver High School before it became a junior high. He graduated from South Carolina State University and served on Spartanburg City Council and in the South Carolina House of Representatives. He is currently serving as a judge in the South Carolina Court of Appeals.

The area was interesting. Even within the housing project, we had a lot of green space; there was grass on the lawns, and we often played at the playground below the old projects. Our area was bounded by "Dog Hollow" and Cemetery Street on one side—those were the older black communities—and on the other side was South Liberty Street, which is where Mount Moriah Church was at that time, and behind us was Duncan Street, it was a nice little area there.

I liked going from one housing project to the other, and I had fun all the way, because you knew everybody in between. The [houses of the] little old ladies, where you'd stop and eat candy … and you sat on the porch with them, and they would ask you about your day and say things like, "Boy, you know I saw you last week, running through here, where had you been? And what had you done?" Then you'd reply, "Oh, not a thing, just playing is all." Then you'd go on down the street and probably throw rocks at a cat or something, those types of things—I enjoyed it.

It was so many people, so many families, so many good people. You always had someone to play with. Of course I had a big family to play with, but there were other kids as well. You could always find a game to play or watch, somewhere, and if you wanted to find trouble, I guess you could find that too. In those days there wasn't much trouble because there were so many other parents always looking out after the children, you couldn't get away with much of anything.

My grandmother, "Ma Maude" we called her, who lived down the street from us, saw everything, and we'd try to sneak out the back way going places we had no business going, and she would see us, and what she didn't see, someone always called her on the phone and told it, so there was no getting into trouble. The neighborhood was like one extended family, and the children of today don't have that, and it's unfortunate.

Perseverance, talking to people, good guidance from my parents, all of these, I attribute to my upbringing and my life as an adult. Some of the people who I think had a big influence on me were Mrs. Taggart, who was a teacher at Carver High, and Dr. Bull. There were others who were very supportive, but not those people whose names you often hear mentioned.

—Interview by Beatrice Hill

Joe Grant

(courtesy, Raymond Floyd)

Joe Grant, the oldest of seven children, was born in 1950, grew up at 291 Tobe Hartwell Extension, and went to Carver High School, Wofford College, and the University of South Carolina. He is currently president of the Grant Group. Here he shares his memory of Tobe Hartwell Apartments and of the civil rights struggle in Spartanburg.

I spent a long time in Tobe Hartwell. What I remember most was believing that living in Tobe was middle class. We had hot and cold running water, indoor toilets, and we thought that was pretty good living. In retrospect, compared to a lot of other people, we were living pretty well. My mother used to make us sweep the yards, scrub the concrete porches, all kinds of things to keep the place clean. The Southside was sort of the center of our world; we didn't know much about anything else. We had very little interaction with white folk because schools were still segregated then, so our interaction with white folk consisted of going to the grocery store or some other minor interacts, but nothing that provided you with the kind of role models and extended support that we got from the south side of town.

It was so easy for me, and others like me to get lost, so it depended on which way the wind was blowing that day. ... We had role models and folk who would reach out and sort of keep you steady. That was important to a young black kid like me, who grew up in the heights of the civil rights struggle, and whose home was without a father.

Dr. Ellen C. Watson was really important to me. She was the guidance counselor at Carver High before going to Spartan High after integration. The kind of attention she paid to me and my siblings helped us to survive. I remember my first set of eyeglasses, her sending me to the Lion's Club. I'd been sitting in class on the front row, not being able to see the bulletin board. I did not know that I needed glasses before Ms. Claiborne Carter sent me to Mrs. Watson who took me to the Lion's Club. My first pair of glasses I wore in my senior class picture, and I've kept them all of these years. I remember coming out of the optometrist office that day and looking around made me realize I really was almost blind. It was amazing. I'll never forget that moment.

Mrs. Watson saw I needed a winter coat. She went out and bought me one. My first trip to Columbia was with her. Those are the kinds of things that people just don't do any more. It was those things that were so important to me, because it was so easy to get lost, and a lot of talented kids who didn't go anywhere for whatever reason, and it was so easy to be in that number.

The fact that I graduated high school and college, and five of my brothers and sisters did the same, is because of role models like Dr. Watson. There was the time when my sister Pearl and a couple of her classmates had graduated high school in 1969, and Dr. Ellen Watson took them to South Carolina State College. She got them jobs in the cafeteria. They didn't have a place to stay because there was no housing available, so she talked one of her old college roommates into letting the girls move in with her on Amelia Street. Those are the kinds of things you do for children if you think they have promise, and if you want to provide an opportunity for them.

It's hard to talk about Mrs. Watson and others like her without getting a little teary-eyed because of (A) you don't see that anymore, and (B) the pride she used to take in standing up in Mount Moriah every Sunday and welcoming home the college kids. Giving us the opportunity to learn to talk to people, how to interact with folk; those types of things were unique to black schools in that period of time.

I came along during the civil rights struggle, so I remember all of the marches, all of the planning for the marches. Our group was organized in marching downtown. … I remember hearing of the threats of the dogs being turned loose on us if we were to cross Main Street. I also remember us at the height of the debate of integrating schools.

We had this major assembly in the gym at Carver High, when the kids decided to walk out on J.G. McCracken, the school superintendent. He struggled to try and talk to us about integration, what that would mean, and our resistance to the idea, our questions about why we couldn't stay in the environment we were in and still have the resources they were putting into white schools, and that what he wanted to say was not what we wanted to hear. We first did an in-school strike, with nobody going to class. All of us assembling in the gym, and Mr. Woodson was struggling with that, and we went home.

Mrs. Watson and others tried to get us back into school and to stay in school. All of that was a part of the frustration over civil rights struggles not moving fast enough because a lot of us thought it was moving slow intentionally. That was when the debate over Malcolm X's method and Martin Luther King's method which was the most effective, and why would you do one and not the other. Martin promoting non-violence and Malcolm promoting a different approach. Lots of us were aspiring to be disciples of Malcolm, because he was more in tune with the impatient attitude that young people had, and Martin's process required a lot more time and a lot of more meeting of the minds.

Malcolm's approach was sort of "in your face," and a lot of us who had a lot of impatience then, as young people do, were quick to aspire to adopt Malcolm's philosophy. But that was a learning process. I chose to go to a white school because I didn't know a lot about white folk, so it was really important to me and others in my class to go away to school and learn how to interact in that society. It became clear the schools were going to be integrated and the community that we had was going to be dissipated through urban renewal and other kinds of things.

—Interview by Beatrice Hill and Brenda Lee

4

Where We Worshipped

~Beatrice Hill~

THE PEOPLE OF AFRICA WERE RELIGIOUS and deeply spiritual long before they came to the Americas, but they found it difficult to preserve their religions under the harsh circumstances of slavery. Many were converted, along with whites, to the Baptist and Methodist denominations during the revivals of the 1780s and 1790s, known as The Great Awakening. During these revivals slaves could worship in the open with whites present. Yet after slave uprisings in the 1820s and 1830s, state legislatures across the South passed laws curtailing the rights of Africans to assemble to worship, fearing that they would plot rebellion against their owners. Many slaves began attending the churches of whites. The published histories of white Spartanburg churches, such as First Baptist and Central Methodist, show a large number of names of black people listed as members.

Most African Americans found their spiritual needs best met in secret. In the slave quarters they often organized their own religious services through signals, passwords, and messages not known to whites. They also established "brush arbors" in wooded places where they mixed African rhythms, singing, and beliefs with evangelical Christianity. In these quiet places they sang spirituals, which embodied their dreams for both religious salvation and freedom from slavery. Early black preachers developed their styles of chanted or rhythmic-style sermons. The first church on the Southside, Mount Moriah Baptist Church on South Liberty, began this way.

In the years after the Civil War the emergence of African-American religious tradition unfolded as slaves were free to organize and worship as they saw fit. Many of them, like the members of Mount Moriah Baptist Church, continued to worship in the brush arbor until a building was provided. Churches in the North encouraged the establishment of missions across the South, such as the Episcopal Epiphany Mission on South Liberty Street, organized at the turn of the century. And by 1894 the black Baptists formed the National Baptist Convention, which now represents the largest black religious organization in the United States.

—MOUNT MORIAH BAPTIST CHURCH—

Mount Moriah Baptist Church had its beginnings in church services that were held in a brush and grape arbor along South Liberty Street, sometime about 1863. Charter members included Joseph Young Sr., who owned the property, and seven others. In 1877 these men made an appeal to the Reverend Vass of Spartanburg's First Baptist Church for aid in building the first edifice at that site, the corner of Young and South Liberty streets.

The first pastors of Mount Moriah were the Reverend Julius Steel and the Reverend W. Murray Evans, though records are not clear which one was first. Much of the church's early history was lost when an early pastor left the church under considerable pressure and took the records with him. More documents were lost when the home of the church secretary caught fire in later years. The Reverend Steel is listed in the 1880 City Directory as one of 17 black men living in a small cluster of homes on South Liberty Street, although

The Reverend H.M. Moore was pastor of Mount Moriah, 1905-1908. This photograph was taken in the early 1920s when he was pastor of Second Calvary Baptist Church in Columbia. The photograph was taken by noted Columbia photographer Richard Samuel Roberts and was included in the book *A True Likeness, The Black South of Richard Samuel Roberts, 1920-1936*.

Evans is listed as the pastor during the years 1878-1888 in the Inventory of Church Archives, collected by the Federal Works Progress Administration in 1936.

On October 13, 1884, Lincoln School opened in the basement of Mount Moriah and became the first graded public school for black children in Spartanburg. The school operated until 1891.

Mount Moriah, Spartanburg's first black Baptist church, spawned two other churches in the area. In 1894 a group left to found Macedonia Baptist Church, and in 1902 another group left to establish Majority Baptist Church.

Mount Moriah Baptist Church, which was organized in 1863, constructed this building in 1914. It was torn down in the 1970s for urban renewal. ~Courtesy, Cheryl Harleston and the City of Spartanburg

The small church built by the Mount Moriah founders was used until 1912, when that building was torn down in order to begin construction of the second Mount Moriah building, which had room for 700 people. During construction the congregation worshiped in a tent across the street and in the Lodge Hall on Liberty Street. The basement of the church was completed in the spring of 1914 and the cornerstone was laid. Services were held in the basement until the upper structure was completed. This church, with its square bell tower and 16 memorial windows, was among the first brick churches built by African-American groups in South Carolina. The contractor was Lucius Gray, brother-in-law to the Reverend J.W. Sexton.

This church housed a large enough sanctuary to accommodate the graduation ceremonies of the local black schools: Carrier Street, Cedar Hill Academy, Dean Street, Cumming Street, and later, Carver High School. The last school graduation was held there in 1950 when the Spartanburg Memorial Auditorium was completed and all of the schools began to use that building for their graduation ceremonies.

Other ministers of the church through the years have included the Rever-

The Reverend and Mrs. Joel L. King are seated in the front row of this photograph from the late 1940s. King was pastor of Mount Moriah Church during the 1940s through the early 1950s. He was an uncle to the late Dr. Martin Luther King Jr. ~Courtesy, Sylvia Nichols

ends H.M. Moore, H.P. Mills, R.W. Baylor, Fletcher Mills, Dr. J.S. Earle, A.M. Matthews, H.P. Pickett, W.S. Colvin, Dr. Joel L. King, and Dr. J. Leon Pridgeon. The current pastor, hired in 1975, is the Reverend Dr. Benjamin D. Snoddy.

Groundbreaking services for the third Mount Moriah Baptist Church were held February 1977, as the former building was torn down in urban renewal. The new church was completed in May 1977 at 445 South Church Street. Under the guidance of Dr. Snoddy, Mount Moriah has built a new Family Life Center, complete with an atrium, chapel, fitness room, gym, classrooms, office, commercial kitchen, and meeting rooms.

✧ This history was collected over the years by Maggie Belle Wheeler, Bessie Scruggs, Lottie Rogers, Ellen Watson, Priscilla Rumley, and Lillie Miller.

A graduation ceremony for Cumming Street High School held at Mount Moriah Baptist Church ~Courtesy, Margaret Finley

J.W. Woodward *(left)* and his son, Stinson Woodward, at the dedication of the new marquee at Mount Moriah Church in 1947. Stinson is the father of Kay Woodward Williams. ~Courtesy, Patricia Nichols

Members of a student band perform at Mount Moriah Church. ~Courtesy, Frances Thompson

The Mount Moriah Baptist Church youth choir in 1959
~Courtesy, Robert Wilson

(below)
A Sunday morning service at Mount Moriah Baptist Church in 1959
~Courtesy, Brenda Lee

—Macedonia Baptist Church—

The Macedonia Baptist Church was organized June 20, 1894, after its members withdrew from Mount Moriah Baptist Church. The church first met in a building located on the corner of South Liberty and East Valley Streets, and the first pastor was the Reverend W.M. Evans. According to church records, the chartered officers were Deacons C.H. Ray, John A. Alston, Arthur Jones, and Dan Jackson. Other recorded members were Emma Rogers and Fannie Foster.

A month later, the small congregation moved to a space above the Wright-Scruggs Shoe Store, which was located in the Andrews Building on Morgan Square. In the fall of 1894 the church family grew and began the search for a new home. A lot was purchased, and a wood building was constructed facing Exchange Street downtown. Macedonia remained at the Exchange Street location from 1896 to 1914.

Subsequent pastors included, in order: the Reverends Wint Wallace, Hemphill, J.M. Brown, C.L. Menefield, J.M. Brown (a second term), J.W. Leake, and John Wallace.

The Reverend E. W. Bowen led the church in the construction of a new edifice in 1914, facing West Henry Street. (That site is now the location of Atchison Plaza.) The Reverend Bowen served until 1920, and the Reverend R.S. Sims was elected as the tenth pastor, serving from 1920 to 1929.

In 1921 Claude Hutchinson, a trustee of the church and a brick mason, helped design and build a new church. The wooden building was used as a basic structure, and the new building was constructed around it. In 1929 the Reverend A. M. Means became pastor and served until 1941. Next was the Reverend Willie L. Wilson in 1942. A new parsonage was purchased at 118 Stribling Circle,

The Reverend John W. Leake was pastor of Macedonia Baptist Church, 1907-1910.
~Courtesy, Brenda Lee

« 89 »

where it remains today.

In view of the urban renewal plans for the West Henry Street area, the members made the decision to build a new edifice at 502 Daniel Morgan Avenue. The first service was held in the new church on the fourth Sunday in November 1983. After 46 years of service at Macedonia, the Reverend Wilson retired in 1988. Deacon Board Chairman Todd Shell retired shortly before the Reverend Wilson, and Deacon Lewis Davis replaced him.

In February 1990 the Reverend Kaiser Jones became pastor, followed by the Reverend Oscar R. Cleveland in October 1999.

The Reverend W.L. Wilson, pastor of Macedonia Baptist Church from the 1940s to the 1970s.

The march to the new sanctuary of Macedonia Church in 1983. In back is Cammie Clagett Courts. ~Courtesy, Cheryl Harleston and the City of Spartanburg

(above) A Sunday School banquet at Macedonia Church, 1947
~Courtesy, Cheryl Harleston and the City of Spartanburg

The old Macedonia Church on West Henry Street ~Courtesy, Cheryl Harleston and the City of Spartanburg

(above) A funeral service at Macedonia Baptist
Church in the 1940s ~Courtesy, Catherine Brannon

The new sanctuary of Macedonia Baptist,
built on Daniel Morgan Avenue in 1983
~Courtesy, Cheryl Harleston and the
City of Spartanburg

—Majority Baptist Church—

In 1902 there were disagreements at Mount Moriah Baptist Church, and a group of members and their families withdrew to organize a new church. Initially they met in members' homes and then moved to a wooden structure on the corner of East Hampton Avenue and South Liberty Street. The members unanimously decided to name themselves Majority Baptist Church.

Noted statesman and counselor the Reverend G. F. Mills helped organize the church and served as its first pastor until his death in 1922. Mills was not only interested in the spiritual needs of the members but also their social and educational needs as well. At that time there was no elementary school in the community for African-American children, so he opened the doors of the little wooden church for children to come and learn to read and write.

The Reverend G. F. Mills, early pastor of Majority Baptist Church

Mills became ill and died as plans were made for the construction of a new edifice. But the congregation continued to raise money for materials while in search of a new pastor. The church called the Reverend T. Elliot Hall in 1924. Unfortunately he met an untimely death, and the church was soon in search of another pastor. The construction of the new church was completed under the tenure of the Reverend J.W. Coleman. The Reverend J.S. Daniels was the fourth pastor and served until his death.

In the early 1950s noted evangelist the Reverend E.A. Davis assumed the responsibility as pastor for a few years before being called away. The year 1956 was the beginning of a new era for Majority when Dr. C.M. Johnson assumed the position of minister. During his 38-year tenure, the church grew spiritually, physically, and financially, and contributed much to the Spartanburg community.

In 1966 the church's educational building was completed and paid for with yearly pledges of the members. Dr. Johnson retired in January of 1994 because of declining health, and in March 1995, the Reverend James Hailstock became pastor. The church purchased the C.C. Woodson home under the Reverend Hailstock's leadership and completed a new church building in 1998 under his guidance.

✧ Contributors to this piece included Patricia Farr, James P. Gilmore, Frieda Johnson, Miller Cunningham, and the late Dr. C. M. Johnson.

The former home of Majority Baptist, built in 1928 ~Courtesy, Cheryl Harleston and the City of Spartanburg

The Deacons Board and pastor of Majority Baptist Church in 1947. *Front row, left to right:* Dennis Smith, Robert E. Osborne, the Reverend J.S. Daniels, M.K. Muckleduff and William Murray. *Second row, left to right:* Pat Anderson, James Rice, B.W. Smith and L.A. Johnson. This photo is from the archives of the Sixty-Ninth Annual Session of the Baptist Educational and Missionary Convention of South Carolina. ~Courtesy, Frank Nichols

Majority's new sanctuary, built in 1983.
~Courtesy, Cheryl Harleston and the City of Spartanburg

A church service at Majority Baptist in the late
1950s ~Courtesy, Frank Nichols

(below) Ushers at Majority Baptist, sometime in
the 1950s ~Courtesy, Frank Nichols

—THE EPISCOPAL EPIPHANY MISSION—

The Episcopal Epiphany Mission was organized in 1893 by the Reverend Theodore D. Bratton, who was the priest of Spartanburg's white Church of the Advent. The Advent's minutes on Palm Sunday of that year indicate that Bratton had inaugurated "a mission among the colored people of the city—the beginning is very modest—a room which is lent for the services serves as a place of worship. This through the kindness of Mrs. Clemons [colored] who has a school in the room [of the Colored Industrial School.]" There were only two confirmed members when the church was organized: William Wanamaker and Perry Young.

A 1940 photograph of the Epiphany Mission, 411 South Liberty.

A permanent home for the Epiphany Mission was built in 1914 at 410 South Liberty Street and operated under the upper South Carolina Diocese. The land on which the church was built was owned by Priscilla Young, who sold it to Bratton in 1897. The first settled clergyman was the Reverend S.W. Grice. The parsonage was built next to the church and doubled as the Epiphany Mission High School. It was a private school for black students. Later, a kindergarten was established in a building behind the mission.

Mary H. Wright established a "Christmas Tree for underprivileged children" at Epiphany, and for many years food and gifts were given to area children and families in the social hall.

Several priests have followed the Reverend Grice, among them, Reverends Bagwell, Simpkins, J.B. Brown, Green, and Robert Long. The Epiphany Mission building stands today in the original location, with only minor renovations over the years.

The Reverend and Mrs. James Brown, 1960. ~Courtesy, the Brown Family

The Reverend and Mrs. James B. Brown *(on left)* and the choir at Epiphany in the early 1940s.

Epiphany Mission in recent times ~Courtesy, Cheryl Harleston and the City of Spartanburg

—Maxwell Chapel Baptist Church—

A small group of people gathered with Julia Epps and the Reverend Tom Foster in a brush arbor on Spartanburg's Southside in 1898 and organized the Possum Trot Church under the Baptist denomination. There were twelve charter members. In 1900 the first church was constructed just east of Duncan Park, off Union Street. In 1929 the church moved to its current location on Duncan Street when Nell Darlington, granddaughter of white landowner J.L. Maxwell, swapped property with the church.

Former pastors included Reverends Yeargin, Dillard, A.M. Matthews, Mac Wallace, Duncan, Stevenson, Zimmerman, White, Posey, L. Snoddy, L. Jackson, M. Jackson, Converse Robinson, and Ogelsby. Two churches have spun off from Maxwell Chapel over the years: New Maxwell Chapel and First Temple.

—Bible Schools—

The Wallace Palmer Mission, a mission of Spartanburg's First Presbyterian Church, opened in 1925 in a building known as the "Old Folk's Home" on Cudd Street. The mission was named for Wallace Palmer, a black minister and gardener well known in the community for his Christian faith and good works. The Bible study class was led by Mary Watkins Carr, a member of First Presbyterian. A children's class soon was added, and, later, the mission built a new location nearby. At one point about 150 pupils were enrolled for classes on Wednesdays and Thursdays. They were called together by a train engine bell given by local railroad executives. In the 1950s this building became the Cudd Street Kindergarten.

An early sketch of "Aunt" Hannah Coln, a beloved early resident of the Southside ~Courtesy, Flander Dunham

Hannah McCaw Coln,

The Hannah Coln Mission began on Byrd Street 1928. "Aunt" Hannah Coln, who had been married to a preacher, offered the use of her home as a way of continuing her husband's work. According to a history of the First Presbyterian Church, eight women were present for the first meeting and soon were joined by other women and their children. For 14 years Mrs. Coln's living room was used for adult classes and her dining room for children's classes.

"Following the class sessions, the floors were often left muddy, for the streets were not paved at that time, and the South Carolina red mud clung to many feet that went in and out of her home every Friday afternoon," according to the Presbyterian Church history. "As the classes grew, the two rooms overflowed, they advanced to one of the bedrooms, and then another bedroom was cheerfully offered."

In 1941, after meeting in this home for 14 years, the First Presbyterian Church erected a building for the Bible classes within a block of Aunt Hannah's home, near Tobe Hartwell Courts. In the 1950s the Hannah Coln Bible School became the Byrd Street Kindergarten.

Members of the
Wallace Palmer
Bible School in
1949

5

Where We Were Educated

~Beatrice Hill~

FORMAL EDUCATION FOR AFRICAN AMERICANS before and during the Civil War was forbidden throughout the South. Many Southern whites believed that education of the slave would spoil him for farm work or other drudgery. However, some African Americans were educated when members of a slave owner's family would befriend their black playmates and secretly teach them how to read. While there was no formal education of black children, historical documents show that there were 1,785 white students in free schools in Spartanburg County in 1860, and many others attended church-supported and private schools.

After emancipation and the end of the Civil War in 1865, African-American common schools began to appear everywhere across the South: in churches, one-room shacks, or wherever black families could gather a group of children and teach them the three R's.

—THE LINCOLN SCHOOL—

After the "Graded School Act" was passed by the South Carolina State Legislature on December 22, 1883, white Spartanburg city leaders formed a citizen's committee and began meeting monthly to discuss public schools, according to a history of Spartanburg School District 7 published by Ella Poats in 1982. The first group of trustees scheduled a meeting to discuss many issues, including plans for a graded school for black children. They suggested that several prominent and influential black citizens, including Tobe Hartwell and Charles Bomar, be invited to sit in on the next meeting. Several offers were made to the committee for the location of the "colored school," including one from the Reverend M. Bethel, who offered the use of the black Presbyterian mission. But in September 1884, the committee decided that the basement of Mount Moriah Baptist Church on South Liberty Street would be the best location.

The committee named Phyllis Bomar, Mary Hartwell, Clara Farrow, and L.B. Lord as the first teachers at the school. The Reverend R.W. Baylor was appointed principal and teacher. The salary was $25 a month for black teachers and $30 for black principals, as compared to $35 for white teachers in other parts of Spartanburg. The committee allocated $250 for laying the floor, making repairs and finishing the church basement in preparation for the school. They purchased 75 double desks with chairs, maps, charts, and blackboards; partitions were placed to divide the lower floor into three rooms, and enough coal-heating

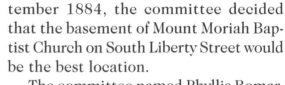

The Reverend Richard W. Baylor, seated, was pastor of Mount Moriah Baptist Church and principal of the Lincoln School in 1884-1888. This photograph was taken much later, in the 1920s, after he had moved to Columbia. His wife, Delphine, is seated at the left, and three of his eight children are standing. From left to right: Walter, Luther, and Bertie. The photograph was taken by noted Columbia photographer Richard Samuel Roberts and was included in the book *A True Likeness, The Black South of Richard Samuel Roberts, 1920-1936.*

stoves were purchased to heat the entire building if needed.

The Lincoln School opened Monday, October 13, 1884, with grades 1-7. Within three months, there was an article in *The Carolina Spartan* that revealed local backlash; some Spartanburg businessmen expressed strong opposition to the common school and to tax dollars being used to educate the poor.

By February 1885 attendance was growing rapidly, and there was a need for more schools. Rendall Academy, located near Wofford and funded by a northern Presbyterian church, was incorporated into the school system and the Reverend W.L. Bethel served as principal. Mrs. N.F. Young was authorized to open a "colored school" at Silver Hill Church, and Sallie Hartwell was her assistant. Then in 1888 Dr. F. Houston, Spartanburg's fourth superintendent of graded schools, began pressing for more suitable school facilities and professionally trained teachers. He oversaw the construction and opening of Dean Street School for black children in 1891, with grades 1-7. With the opening of Dean Street, the Lincoln School and all of the other church schools supported by the city school system were closed.

—THE COLORED INDUSTRIAL TRAINING SCHOOL—

The Colored Industrial Training School opened around 1891 in a building on Clement Street on the Southside. (The new Mary H. Wright Elementary School now occupies that space). Thomas A. J. Clemons, a black man who lived in the area, was principal, and there were three teachers. Not supported by the public school system, the Training School survived by making appeals to the public and receiving donations from individuals and organizations. These donations included funds ranging from fifty cents to $500, as well as boxes of clothing, shoes, hymnals, prayer books, papers, and magazines. In the 1891-92 school year, the school taught and trained 168 children, including 30 orphans. The boys did carpentry and bricklaying and learned to frame chairs and to make shuck collars and willow baskets. For the girls, there were classes in cooking, sewing and general housekeeping. Students who could afford it paid $6 a month in room and board.

In May 1892, the school issued a pamphlet called "Annual Report of the Colored Industrial Training School," that was sent to churches across the North-east, seeking donations to support day-to-day operations and construction of a new school building. In that pamphlet, now on file at the U.S. Library of Congress, Clemons describes his school's academic curriculum of arithmetic, geography, grammar, history, and literature, as well as vocal and instrumental music. "So the colored people of Spartanburg, S.C., banded together as they are in educating the Negroes of this section, both intellectually and educationally," he wrote in the pamphlet, "and it is our intention to train step by step until we shall reach the high plain of civilization, right, and Christianity."

History is not clear about how many years the school lasted, but it was closed by the end of the century.

—THE EPIPHANY EPISCOPAL MISSION SCHOOL—

The Epiphany Episcopal Mission School began in downtown Spartanburg on Wall Street in 1893, with Southside residents Mary Wright and her sister Clara F. Young as teachers and S. J. Poiner as Lay Leader. Four years later the church-supported school moved to South Liberty Street and eventually was housed behind Epiphany Church. Although not supported by the city school system, this private school survived for about 30 years.

Harriet Dawkins, born in 1907, remembers the early years of this school, when it was named The Bagwell School, after the Reverend Bagwell, who ran it. "The Reverend Bagwell and his family were there," she said in an interview. "In those days the congregation was only a few people. The salary for Reverend Bagwell came from the money he and his family made from selling nice clothes to the public that were sent here from the (Episcopal) mission up North. I have worn many dresses bought at their sidewalk sales."

A photograph from the Mary Wright family archives shows an early 20th century school group. This presumably is the school building that both served as the Colored Industrial Training School and the elementary schoolhouse, founded by Mary Wright, which preceded Carrier Street School. ~Courtesy, Frances Thompson

—Mary H. Wright and Carrier Street School—

With Dean Street School being the only public elementary school for blacks in the city of Spartanburg, Southside children had to walk from one side of town to the other. Many people considered this distance far too long for smaller children. Mary H. Wright was worried that children on the Southside would not get an education, and in 1904 she began teaching children in her home on South Liberty Street. Soon thereafter Mayor John F. Floyd authorized the use of the abandoned Colored Industrial Training School for this school, and Mrs. Fannie D. Young was appointed Mrs. Wright's assistant. In 1906 the city school system began funding the school.

An early 1900s image of Carrier Street School and its student body.

By 1907 the students of Mary Wright had outgrown their temporary school, and it was torn down in order to build another one. In the meantime, Majority Baptist Church opened its doors, and Mary Wright taught her classes there until the new school was built. Carrier Street School opened in 1908 with grades 1-7, and in four rooms. In 1912 the building was expanded to eight rooms. Asa Thompson served as first principal, followed by H. Liston, C.C. Woodson Sr., and Milton Harris. Carrier Street was located where the new Mary H. Wright Elementary School is now, and was known for the May Day programs held on the campus, with the wrapping of the Maypole.

Carrier Street School 7th grade graduating class, about 1940. The principal, seated at center, was Milton Harris. ~Courtesy, Kitty Collins Tullis

Among the Cedar Hill students in this historic 1924 photograph are: Eddie Tucker, Leroy Tucker, Margaret Moore Finley, Ernest Collins, Stinson Woodward, Rossie Sexton, Madge Young Williams, Ansel Perry, Abbie Helen Earle, Reba Martin, Alma Downs, Walter Blakeley, Columbus Moore, Edith Will Duffie, Willie James Blakeley, Willie Yeargin, Grady Yeargin, Hallie Nesbitt, Katherine Mayberry, Ruth Earle, James Earle, Kenneth Brewton, Helen Sexton, Lula Bell Sexton, Johnnny Sexton, Anease Bryant, Lois Brewton, Pauline Bryant Brewton and Louise Coker, George Nichols, and Frank Nichols Sr. Teachers (*seated in front*) are: Azzie McGee, Miss Brewton, the Reverend J. S. Earle, Mrs. Brewton and Mr. Brewton. ~Courtesy, Madge Young Williams

—CEDAR HILL ACADEMY—

In the 1906-07 year Superintendent Frank Evans ended the teaching of algebra and Latin in the black public schools and instead added industrial training. The boys were taught carpentry, and the girls, laundering and sewing. This change angered parents in the black community and helped spur the establishment of Cedar Hill Academy on the Southside in 1915. Partially funded by a group called the Tiger River Association, Cedar Hill served grades 6-11 and was founded by the Reverend J.S. Earle, then pastor of Mount Moriah Church, and a few of his deacons, including Lonnie Holoman. Cedar Hill was a private boarding and day school for black children, where algebra and Latin were a part of the curriculum. Parents paid tuition, and often room and board, for their children to attend Cedar Hill. Students came from across South and North Carolina as well as from Spartanburg. The school was located on a site where Carver Junior High School now stands.

Margaret Moore Finley, born in 1913, began attending Cedar Hill in the sixth grade. "I remember the May Day celebrations as one of my favorite activities, where we had to wrap the pole with different colored streamers, and Ms. McGee would play the music on the piano." She was a day student and had chores to do after school. "There were classrooms on the bottom floor and the boarding students were upstairs," she remembered. "We only had about five or six teachers there, but Mrs. Earle was my favorite because she paid the tuition for me to go to Cedar Hill. There were about eight students in my graduation class, and I was the valedictorian."

In 1926 the Spartanburg School System opened Cumming Street School near Wofford College, with grades 1-9. Many of the parents of the local children who were attending Cedar Hill began sending their children to the free public school instead. Consequently, by the late 1920s Cedar Hill was suffering from a lack of funding. By 1931 the building was deserted and later burned down. (Carver High School was later built on the same lot.)

—KINDERGARTENS—

Kindergartens began to appear on the Southside in the late 1930s, starting with the Cudd Street Kindergarten, spearheaded by the First Presbyterian Church. The Presbyterians later also helped fund the nearby Byrd Street Kindergarten. In the mid-1940s the Epiphany Episcopal parsonage was reopened as a kindergarten by Cornelia Young and lasted many years.

Graduation 1955 at the kindergarten of the Church of the Epiphany. Teachers that year were: Father Green and Frances Holcombe on the left, and Cornelia Young, right.
~Courtesy, Brenda Lee

(above) The kindergarten class at Episcopal Church of the Epiphany, 1948-1949 ~Courtesy, Jacqualine Farr Douglas

A "Tom Thumb Wedding" at Cudd Street Kindergarten in the 1940s ~Courtesy, Betty Payden

The kindergarten class of Byrd Street School in 1969 ~Courtesy, Beatrice Hill

—CARVER HIGH SCHOOL—

Carver High School, "Pride of the Southside," opened on South Liberty Street in 1938, with grades 8-11. C.C. Woodson Jr. was principal throughout most of its history as a high school. He was known to run a tight ship and was highly respected in the community. Carver, through the years, had a faculty that inspired and led students in the study of English, math, and sciences, catapulting many black Spartanburg residents into professional careers. Through necessity, its educators adopted all kinds of innovative methods to educate Spartanburg's black teenagers. During this era of Jim Crow and racial segregation, the textbooks often were hand-me-downs. Teachers regularly brought magazines and newspapers into the classrooms because they were not a staple in students' homes.

Former students describe how Carver High was an institution that reflected the drive of people to escape poverty and second-class living status. Teachers did not back away from the students: they demanded, got, and gave respect, and they insisted on discipline. The teachers, coaches, and administrators at Carver held high expectations of their students in academics and extracurricular activities. Carver was a AAA high school in athletics, and its teams excelled in basketball, football, and track, among other sports, winning trophies, awards, and ribbons.

Many people remember the school parades at homecoming and Christmas, when the drum major and the majorettes would dance in unison to the music of the band stepping behind them. The

The Carver Alma Mater

Oh, Carver High, dear Carver High,
Your name to us will never die.
Tho' years may pass, and classes go,
 your name we'll praise, forevermore.

We'll always wave our banners gay,
where garnet-gray do nobly lay;
When from thee each has gone away,
we will for thee strive hard each day.

Oh, Carver High, dear Carver High,
You stand for truth, both firm and right.
So still the hand of memories light,
Shine proudly in our hearts with heights.

The Alma Mater was composed by teachers Flora Powell and Louvenia Barksdale and was sung to the tune of "Sweet Genevieve."

Recess at Carver High, 1947 ~Courtesy, Margaret Santiago

Carver students in 1947 learning the art of bricklaying.
Their instructor was J.C. Abercrombie.

spectacular performance went all the way down Main Street, as Carver's band entertained the crowds of both black and white spectators gathered on the sidewalks in anticipation of the event.

Among the memorable teachers at Carver were Joseph Lyles, Miller Cunningham, William Clemons, Geraldine Cureton, George Swindler, Lola Taggart, Patricia Alexander, Janie Cooper, Waddell Pearson, Roy Henderson, John Abercrombie, and Albert Campbell. There were many others, and they left lasting impressions on the thousands of students that came through their classroom doors.

In 1970 schools in Spartanburg County were integrated, and Carver became a junior high in 1971, serving both black and white students. In 2001, the old Carver building was torn down to make way for a more modern junior high campus on the Southside.

(below) Three students from Carver High, 1948. The USO is in the background. ~Courtesy, Margaret Santiago

Camillus C. Woodson Jr. became principal of Carver High School when it opened in 1938. He attended Carrier Street and Dean Street elementary schools and completed his high school and undergraduate work at Benedict College, putting himself through school as a Pullman porter and hotel waiter. He studied the insurance business in Philadelphia and became an assistant file supervisor for one of the largest black insurance companies in the United States. In 1932 he became principal of Cumming Street School in Spartanburg. This photograph appeared in the 1947 Carver Tiger annual.

James "Yank" Thompson was captain of the Carver football team in 1946.

The Big Four

If you went to Carver High School, you remember "the Big Four." Louvenia D. Barksdale, Ellen C. Watson, Flora W. Powell, and Claiborne E. Carter, were all, in their own ways, outstanding, remarkable, and powerful women who wanted, demanded, received, and gave the best for their students. They worked hard to make sure their students were well prepared for higher education after high school graduation so that they could become responsible citizens of the community.

Louvenia D. Barksdale (1913-1990)

A prominent English teacher for 37 years in Spartanburg County schools, Ms. Barksdale's teaching career began at Carver in the late 1930s and ended at Spartanburg High School in the 1970s. She worked hard to help students continue their education after high school. A stern woman, Ms. Barksdale made her students believe they could achieve their goals in life. One of her greatest accomplishments was the creation of the Louvenia Barksdale Sickle Cell Foundation in Spartanburg in 1974.

Ellen C. Watson (1916-1990)

Considered one of the most notable of all Carver High teachers, Ellen Watson began as a home economics teacher and later became a guidance counselor. She encouraged talented students to pursue a college education and made great efforts to help them, including often writing checks to pay for their college application fees. Her 41-year career was full of many achievements. She became the first black director of guidance counseling services in Spartanburg School District 7. In 1982 a public housing complex was named in her honor.

Flora W. Powell

Flora Powell, senior English teacher and music director, was known for being one of the strictest disciplinarians to ever come through Carver High. When one of her students was not progressing as she knew he or she could, she would utter one of her favorite sayings: "You may January, and you may February, but you sure won't March." That statement usually steered the student back on track.

Claibourne E. Carter (1912-1989)

Claibourne Carter was senior class teacher of American and world history and also taught physical education. She touched many lives in her 42 years of teaching, inspiring her students to achieve their best. Carter was the first girls' basketball coach at Carver High School. After winning 23 consecutive games, she led the girls' varsity basketball teams to win the AAA State Championship in 1959.

—Beatrice Hill

The Big Four

Former Carver High School Teachers

Louvenia Delores Barksdale

Junior English

Ellen Carter Watson

Home Economics, Foods, Dean of Girls

Flora Wallace Powell

Senior English, Music Directress

Claibourne Eugenia Carter

Social Sciences, Physical Education

(above) James Campbell was president of the band in 1947. Other members included Charles Clowney, James A. Suber, Charlie Nelson, Elmore Bobo, Leroy Simpson, Rosebrough Smith, and Robert Massey.

The Carver junior varsity basketball team, 1959 ~Courtesy, James Gilchrist

Band members at Carver, 1958
~Courtesy, Brenda Lee

Mrs. Althea
Amos's Latin class
at Carver High
School in about
1960 ~Courtesy,
Brenda Lee

Junior High School members of Carver's Junior Honor Society in the mid-1960s ~Courtesy, the James Jones family

Carver High School Seniors Awards Day, 1959 ~Courtesy, James Jones family

Carver senior class, 1948 ~Courtesy, Margaret Santiago

(below) Carver High School teachers in the mid-1950s ~Courtesy, Beatrice Hill

Carver High School sophomores in 1960. Standing *(left to right):* Joyce Patterson, Petunia Posey, Mary Goss, Sara Shelton, Geraldine Cureton. *Seated:* Sandra Gray, Patricia Montgomery, Dorothy Edwards, Emma Taylor, Gloria Hailey. ~Courtesy, Patricia Montgomery

Carver, shortly before its demolition ~Courtesy, *Spartanburg Herald-Journal*

—MARY H. WRIGHT ELEMENTARY—

Mary H. Wright Elementary School opened for the 1951-52 school year on Caulder Avenue, with grades 1-6, and was named for the legendary Southside educator. Charlie B. Hauser served as first principal. The building is now used for adult education, while the new Mary H. Wright Elementary shares the campus grounds with Carver Junior High.

Charlie Mae Campbell was principal of
Mary H. Wright Elementary School for 30 years.
~Courtesy, Cheryl Harleston and the City of Spartanburg

Edith Duffie, a teacher at Mary H. Wright School
~Courtesy, Cheryl Harleston

—OTHER PUBLIC SCHOOLS WE ATTENDED—

Although it was not located on the Southside, many neighborhood residents attended Dean Street School, which opened in 1891 to serve black children in grades 1-7. This was the first structure built in Spartanburg County for the purpose of public education for black children. Soon, an eighth grade class was added.

The first class of black students graduated from the eighth grade of Dean Street School in 1898. They were Catherine McNeil, Drayton H. Nance, Gussie L. Gaither, Samuel Wiggins, Joseph H. Bomar, and Thomas Edwards. While the tenth grade was added to white Spartanburg schools by 1907, Dean Street remained at the eighth grade level. In the 1915-16 school year, white schools added the eleventh grade, and shortly after that, Dean Street advanced to the ninth grade.

In 1939, with the opening of Carver High, Dean Street was changed to Alexander Elementary School for black children. Dean Street School still stands in Spartanburg, now occupied by the Omega Fraternity.

Cumming Street School opened behind Wofford College in 1926 for black students in grades 1-9. In the 1930s, shortly before Carver High opened, Cumming added 10th and 11th grades. W.P. Dendy, who formerly was principal at Cedar Hill, served as principal at Cumming Street in 1928-31. This school closed in 1982 and now serves as headquarters for the Baptist Association of Spartanburg County.

Highland Elementary opened in 1915 on West Henry Street (now the site of Snyder Motor Co.), serving black children on the southwestern side of the city. Milton Harris served as the first principal. When Highland opened in 1915, the students from the privately-run Hamburg school (1912-15), located in a big house on Thompson Street, transferred there. Mrs. L.D. Frazier was the first principal at the Hamburg school.

After Carrier Street Elementary was torn down in the 1950-51 school year, students from the Southside went to Highland for a year in anticipation of the opening of Mary H. Wright.

Students from Dean Street School across town. This photograph was taken in 1924. Charlie Mae Campbell, who became principal of Mary Wright Elementary is in the top row, second from right. Farrow Belle McWhirter, Mary Wright's granddaughter, is in the fourth row, second from right. ~Courtesy, Frances Thompson

⟡6

Residents
at Mid-Century

"*On those streets there was a spirit,
a kind of good feeling in the air. …
We had a sense of togetherness,
and a sense of helping each other
and that sort of thing. People
looked out for each other.*"

—Dewey Tullis

Photograph of Arthur Sessum, taken in 1945
~Courtesy, the Gilchrist Family

Rebecca Smith lived on East Park Drive. She was a cook at
Mary H. Wright Elementary School in its early days.
~Courtesy, Loretta Nash

This is a 1957 driver's license belonging to Rome
Pyles, born in 1902 on Pyles Street. Pyles was a
chauffer and butler, who died in 1965. He and his wife,
Lannie, had one child, Bennie Mae Pyles Bell.
~Courtesy, Pat Whittenburg

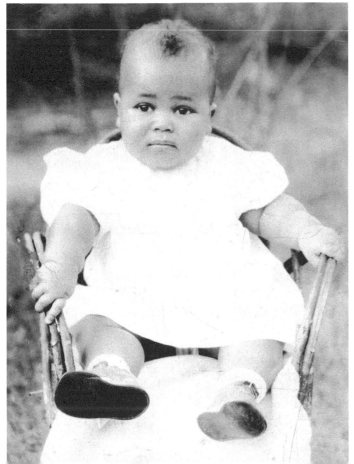

(above) Barbara Montgomery, photographed on Young Street in 1949 ~Courtesy, Barbara Collier

(top left) Ann Montgomery poses in her front yard at 177 Young Street in 1943. The three houses in the background, left to right, were the homes of Agnes Jones, Corrie Caldwell, and Mamie Grant. ~Courtesy, Barbara Collier

(bottom left) Thelma Wofford, a niece of Lannie and Rome Pyles, 1935 ~Courtesy, Pat Whittenburg

Irene Worthy *(center)* babysitting her siblings

(right) Louise Harriston was housekeeper for the Collins family at their home on South Liberty Street. This photo dates from the early 1940s. ~Courtesy, Kitty Collins Tullis

(far right) Joe Cannon and Deb Bonds on the steps of their home on Sydney Street in June 1957 ~Courtesy, Irene Bonds

Twin brothers Harry and Larry Campbell at their grandmother's house in October 1954 ~Courtesy, the Campbell family

A neighborhood birthday party in 1952. Standing, *left to right:* Elizabeth Freeman, Donald Palmer, Cynthia Davis, Brenda Lee, Dorthene Williams. Seated, Diane Wright, Ann Lee, Martha Wright, Sharon Davis, and Charles Foster. ~Courtesy, Brenda Lee

Emma Collins, sitting on the bumper in a white coat, along with her friends at Collins Service Station.
Helen Bobo is on the right. ~Courtesy, Kitty Collins Tullis

A Collins Transportation bus driver and two soldiers from Camp Croft. Collins regularly transported the soldiers at the base to businesses on the Southside. ~Courtesy, Cheryl Harleston and the City of Spartanburg

(top right) Collins employees clear snow from the street in preparation for heading to Camp Croft. ~Courtesy, Cheryl Harleston and the City of Spartanburg

(right) A photographic portrait taken in the late 1940s of Althea and Colonel Robert Amos. Mrs. Amos was a teacher at Highland Elementary and Carver High. Mr. Amos retired from the armed services and then was hired by the Housing Authority as director of Tobe Hartwell in the 1950s. ~Courtesy, the Amos family

Members of the African-American 240 Ordnance Ammunition Co. were stationed at Camp Croft in 1944. Members of this company made frequent trips to the USO Club at 625 South Liberty Street in Spartanburg, formerly the home of the Preston family. The building had a game room, soda fountain, a lounge area and a dance room that was used for frequent parties. Alcoholic beverages were not permitted. ~Courtesy, Jessie Sanders

Ella Prysock and her family lived on South Liberty Street before their home was purchased to make room for the C.C. Woodson Recreation Center. Ella was the mother of Andrew Prysock. ~Courtesy, Andrew Prysock

Patricia Montgomery and Effie Rochell at 177 Young Street in April 1957 ~Courtesy, Barbara Collier

Edith Duffie in her yard on South Liberty Street. This photo dates from about 1955. ~Courtesy, Gertrude and Harry Campbell

(bottom left) Jessie Moore at her home on Young Street in 1940 ~Courtesy, Jessie Sanders

Farrow Belle McWhirter and a friend.
~Courtesy, Frances Thompson

Barbara Montgomery with her
uncle Jesse Montgomery on
Young Street in 1940
~Courtesy, Barbara Collier

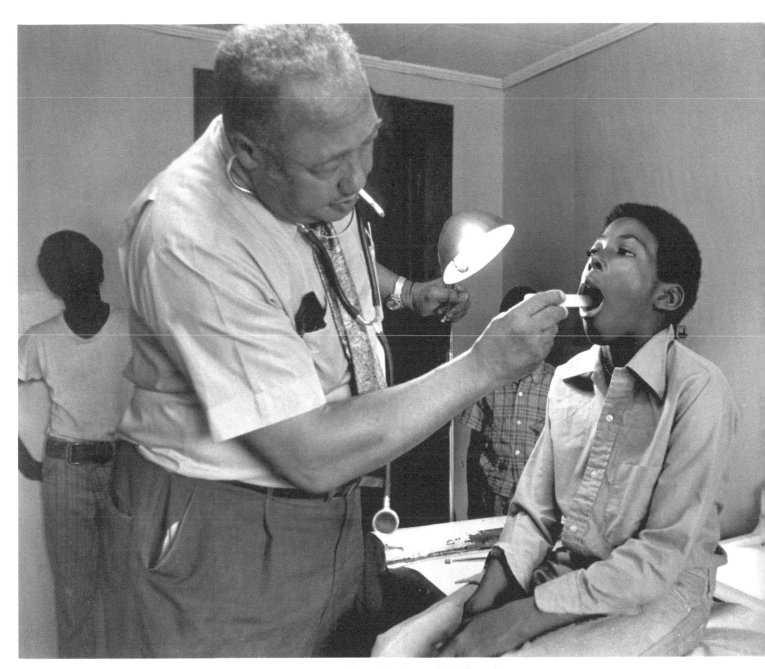

Dr. John Capus (J.C.) Bull sees a patient at his office on South Liberty Street.
~Courtesy, Cheryl Harleston and the City of Spartanburg

James Herrington Young, born in 1884, moved to Spartanburg from Columbia around 1930. Young was a stonemason and bricklayer who graduated from Add's Masons, and Graham and Emory School in New York. He was skilled in tile setting and blueprinting. Some of his stonework can be seen at the American Legion in Duncan Park, which he did in a WPA Project. He was married to Octavia Young, and their daughter is Annie Young Gordon.
~Courtesy, Annie Young Gordon

(above) Sisters Janie Gault and Georgia Gault and their friend, Nellie Patterson, 1949
~Courtesy, the Hollis family

Flora Lyles lived at 148 Carrier Street. This photograph was made in 1963.
~Courtesy, Barbara Collier

Frank Nichols Jr. on Cudd Street in 1950. He served in World War II and was a bricklayer. ~Courtesy, Frank Nichols Jr.

(top right) Beatrice Hill, Patricia Hackett, and Grace Norman *(left to right)* during recess at Carver High in 1957 ~Courtesy, Beatrice Hill

Pervas "Dink" Switzer delivered ice to homes in the 1940s and 1950s. ~Courtesy, Kitty Collins Tullis

Matthew Perry:
U.S. District Court Judge

For ten years during the thick of the Jim Crow era in South Carolina, Matthew Perry practiced law from a small office on South Liberty Street in Spartanburg. From there, he would rise to become what one scholar in a new biography has described as "the Palmetto State's Thurgood Marshall."

Perry was born in Columbia and served in Europe during World War II. In 1951 he graduated from the South Carolina State College Law School, and his family encouraged him to move to Spartanburg, according to his 2004 biography, *Matthew J. Perry: The Man, His Time and His Life*, edited by W. Lewis Burke and Belinda F. Gergel. By living in Spartanburg, he was following in the footsteps of Arthur Chester Platt, the only other black South Carolinian ever admitted to law practice by the South Carolina Bar Association. Platt, who lived on the north side of Spartanburg, represented black-owned North Carolina Mutual Life Insurance Co. and was a member of the state bar from 1922 until he retired in 1942. When young Matthew Perry cast his gaze toward Spartanburg, Platt's widow offered to donate her husband's law library to him. And so at age 30, Perry and his wife, Hallie Bacote, moved into a house on the Southside. He opened a one-room office on South Liberty Street with an Underwood typewriter and a new briefcase, according to his biography.

Business was slow for Perry in Spartanburg—most blacks preferred to hire white lawyers who stood a better chance with white judges and juries—so Perry spent time studying the court decisions across the United States that were challenging the Jim Crow system of segregation. He quickly built a statewide reputation as a keen legal mind and a champion of civil rights for African Americans.

While living in Spartanburg in 1954 Perry took on the case of Sarah Mae Flemming, a black woman in Columbia who alleged that after she refused to move to the back of a public bus, the driver hit her in the stomach. A year before the landmark Rosa Parks case in Montgomery, Alabama, Perry argued in court that segregation on public transportation was illegal. Although he and his partner, Lincoln Jenkins, lost the case in South Carolina, they assisted on the appeal as NAACP lawyers took it to the U.S. Supreme Court. Perry's client eventually won the case, though forced integration of buses went unheeded across the South for several years.

Once, during his years in Spartanburg, a cross was burned on his lawn, he said in an interview published in his biography.

In the late 1950s he chaired the legal committee of the South Carolina NAACP. By then he had made a reputation as a passionate advocate for civil rights for black people and was beginning to handle high-profile cases throughout South Carolina. After the Sarah Mae Flemming case, Perry went on to defend black civil rights demonstrators across the state, including those who carried out lunch counter sit-ins in Greenville, Sumter, Charleston, and Rock Hill. He also represented Charleston teenager Harvey Gantt in his successful 1961 lawsuit to integrate Clemson University. Perry left Spartanburg in 1961 and moved to Columbia, where he went on to have an illustrious legal career.

Appointed by President Jimmy Carter in 1979, Perry became the first African American named U.S. District Court Judge in South Carolina's history and, in 1995, achieved senior status. In 2004 the Matthew J. Perry Jr. United States Courthouse in Columbia was dedicated in his honor. He continues to live and work in Columbia.

—Betsy Teter

Mattie Montgomery in her kitchen at 148 Carrier Street in 1959
~Courtesy, Barbara Collier

(bottom left) Macie Irene Coln Dunham, born 1887, was the oldest child of Hannah Coln. ~Courtesy, Flander Dunham

(below) Jessie Moore Sanders, who grew up on Young Street, poses with some friends in about 1945. She is on the right.
~Courtesy, Jessie Sanders

Just across South Church Street were the homes of many white Spartanburg families. Here are Idella and Linda Bearden at 118 Milster Street in December 1943. South Church Street is in the background. ~Courtesy, Polly Bearden Bennett

Polly Bearden on Milster Street in 1943.
The street at that time was unpaved.
~Courtesy, Polly Bearden Bennett

On a Sunday afternoon in 1947, Minnie Carter Montgomery (1875-1956) and Flora Woodward Lyles (1885-1966) posed at the former's house at 177 Young Street with their grandchildren after services at Mt. Moriah Baptist Church. Left to right are Anne Montgomery (1940-1995), Minnie C. Montgomery, Patricia Montgomery (1945-), Flora W. Lyles, and Barbara Montgomery (1937-). Anne later taught in a literacy program for adults, Patricia taught high school in Charlotte, and Barbara assisted elderly patients with Alzheimer's disease. ~Courtesy, Damon Fordham

A photograph of Mr. and Mrs. Thomas Young, who lived on the Southside. Though he was small, Thomas Young served as a custodian at City Hall.

(right) Newman Brown and a friend working on a Collins bus ~Courtesy, the Reverend James Brown family

In the 1940s Mary H. Wright *(standing second from the right)* started a chapter of the American Red Cross at the newly opened Tobe Hartwell Apartments. Her eldest daughter, Addie, is at left. ~Courtesy, Frances Thompson

Waddell Pearson in 1946 in
his World War II naval uniform.
He became a teacher and
coach at Carver High School.
~Courtesy, Brenda Lee

Ted Wright playing with his band in 1956 ~Courtesy, the Wright family

(left) Ted Wright, at the piano, played at local hotels and clubs in the 1940s and '50s. Born in Abbeville, he moved to the Southside at a young age. He played at the Blue Lantern on South Liberty, as well as many segregated white clubs such as the Piedmont Club, the Spartanburg County Club, the Franklin Hotel and the Police Club. Known for his piano playing and smooth voice on versions of popular jazz songs, he also played radio shows on WSPA-AM. During the 1960s Ted played at the Robin Hood Club, a popular night spot for blacks on the Southside. Among his band members were Donald Ezell of Spartanburg on bass fiddle, Bill Dover on trumpet and Reed Sullivan on drums, both of Greenville; and Elmer, from Germany on bass fiddle. Ted was born in 1919 and died in 1973. ~Courtesy, the Wright family

Stella Ezell Coln in her living room on
Clement Street in 1952. Married to
Ernest Coln, she was the grandmother
to Brenda Lee. ~Courtesy, Brenda Lee

John "Slim" Smith, husband of Rebecca Smith, in his yard
on East Park Avenue in 1947 ~Courtesy, the Smith family

Willie B. Wilson, a soldier in World War II, 1943
~Courtesy, Beatrice Hill

Members of VFW Post 9349 gather on Memorial Day in 1950 at Mount Moriah Church. "Buck" Campbell is kneeling at bottom right. Next to him is Sam Freeman. Bessie Mae Wofford is standing in the dark dress at left. This post was chartered in 1947 by a few black war veterans from Spartanburg and originally met in members' houses. Later, they used the upstairs of a club owned by McKinnley "Booster" Palmer on South Liberty. The post was named for Edward J. Lindsey, a Spartanburg soldier killed during the war. After a few years the post moved to a building owned by Dr. J.C. Bull on Caulder Circle, where it remains. ~Courtesy, Beatrice Hill

Brothers, Charles and Roosevelt Stewart, 1950 ~Courtesy, Charles Stewart

In 1956 George Woodward became the city's first black disk jockey at WJAN ("With Jive At Night"), which broadcast from the first floor of the Schuyler Building on South Church Street. He was known for his hip phrases at the beginning of his show, called "George Hot Spot." Later he went to work at WTHE "on the banks of the mighty Chinquapin" near the former Gas Bottom neighborhood. ~Courtesy, George Woodward

Woodward eventually went to the popular WORD station, where he invited his listeners to come for a ride on the "Night Train." In addition to his radio programs, he managed two record shops, one on South Liberty and the other on Saint John, where he sold the latest records of rhythm and blues, gospel, and other artists. ~Courtesy, George Woodward

Ernest Collins and his wife, Emma, in the early days of their transportation business~Courtesy, Ernestine Collins Anderson

Ada Bagwell Foster was principal of Dean Street School. She and her husband, Walter Foster, lived at the corner of South Dean and Henry Streets from 1937 until urban renewal in the 1970s. ~Courtesy, Rosalind Brown

Kitty Collins Tullis holds Joseph "Joey" Patton III in this photograph from the early 1940s. Patton was the son of the neighborhood barber, Joe Patton. ~Courtesy, Rosalind Brown

This photograph was made on August 11, 1946, on Mary H. Wright's 85th birthday. Mary, seated, died two weeks later. ~Courtesy, Frances Thompson

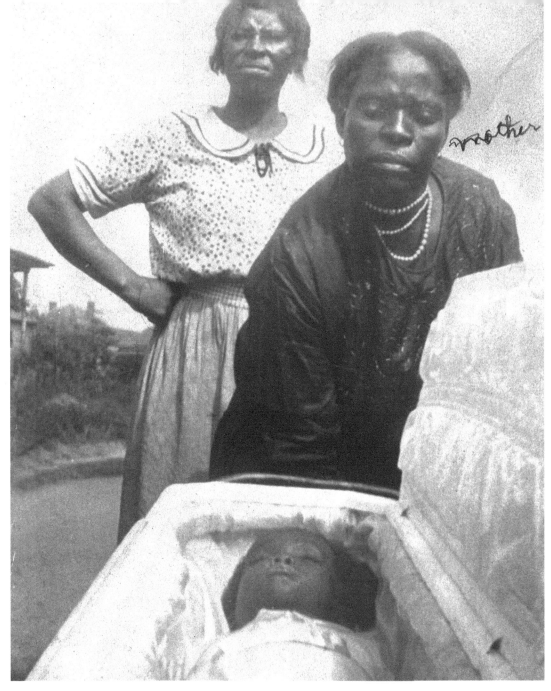

mother

Pearl Roebuck *(back)* and her stepmother, Lula Roebuck, at a wake for a neighborhood child who choked to death about 1940. It was customary at the time to bring the deceased home for a wake before he or she was buried. At the time of this photograph, Pearl was a laundress and lived with her family, Lula and William Roebuck, at 345 Cudd Street. Pearl later worked for more than three decades at Pine Street School, eventually becoming superintendent of the custodial staff. She died in 1994 at the age of 88. ~Courtesy, James Roebuck

Will Prysock, husband of Ella Prysock, and their grandson, Harrison
~Courtesy, Andrew Prysock

A photograph of Sandy Warren, taken in 1947
~Courtesy, the Gilchrist family

Marie Dickert at her home on South Liberty Street in 1950
~Courtesy, the Campbell family

(right) Rosalind Patton and her brother, Joey, are standing in the center of East Henry Street near the intersection with South Dean in this photograph from 1951. In the back is a railroad track which once crossed Main Street, and the homes of Elford Terrace. The Patton family later moved to a home on Elford Terrace.
~Courtesy, Rosalind Brown

Charles Norwood, a resident of East Hampton Avenue, and Boyd Cheeks were photographed together in the late 1940s. Cheeks was a baker for many years for Quality Bakery, 184 East Main Street. He lived in Tobe Hartwell.
~Courtesy, Ruth Jeffries

Arthur Prysock

Pop crooner and balladeer Arthur Prysock was born on the Southside January 2, 1929. As a recording artist with Decca Records, then Old Time, he released several memorable R&B albums between the years 1952 and 1987.

Although he moved to Greensboro, North Carolina, at the age of three, Prysock made frequent trips with his brother, "Red," back to Spartanburg to help his grandfather on the family cotton farm. As a teenager he stayed with his uncle, Shafter Mills, in Spartanburg for some time, according to an interview published in *Cadence*, a jazz journal. Members of the Prysock family still live in Spartanburg.

At age 15, Arthur Prysock moved to Hartford, Connecticut, and joined the Buddy Johnson blues band as lead vocalist, playing clubs in Harlem and

Arthur Prysock during his years with the Buddy Johnson Orchestra ~Courtesy, Joan Mills recording albums. In 1952 he began a solo career and often toured with his brother Wilbert "Red" Prysock, a noted saxophonist.

His first hit record was "I Didn't Sleep a Wink Last Night," in 1952, followed by "The Very Thought of You" in 1960 and "It's Too Late, Baby, It's Too Late" in 1965. He also had a surprise disco hit in 1985, "When Love is New." Prysock was also known for singing the well-known TV ad jingle, "Tonight, Let It Be Lowenbrau," and in 1986 had a hit with "This Guy's in Love with You."

Arthur Prysock died June 7, 1997. Red Prysock died in 1993.

Wilbert "Red" Prysock, brother of Arthur, was a prominent saxophone player who visited his family on the Southside often.

7

Places We Remember

"It's such a broad memory, it's almost impossible to bring it down to one particular spot. When I think about it, I see this mural of things that happened on the Southside. I'd see myself walking down Liberty Street, passing each business there."

—James Talley

(above) The Atchison vehicle lot, 362 South Liberty Street, in the 1960s ~Courtesy, Cheryl Harleston and the City of Spartanburg

The home of the Reverend James Brown, pastor at the Episcopal Mission, on East Valley Street ~Courtesy, the Reverend Brown family

Candy Stripers and their friends pose for a picture at the Recreation Center in February 1959. Left to right: Zenobia Jackson, Robert McKissick, an unidentified woman, Trutella Fuller, Carrie Edwards, and Sylvia Evans ~Courtesy, Brenda Lee

Charles Atchison's "Checker Cab," 1964 ~Courtesy, Cheryl Harleston and the City of Spartanburg

"Our house on Liberty Street was a modest but comfortable one. During the early part of the war, the local newspaper was doing a survey on black neighborhoods' living conditions. They took a picture of our house, and the article said it was the most modern in that neighborhood. I remember there was a cafe called Po Boy's Lunch, and as kids we used to go there and eat and dance after school. All of the proms and basketball games were at the T.K. Gregg Center, because Carver didn't have a gym at that time. I also remember the Blue Lantern. It was sort of a recreation spot, and further up was the Episcopal Church. The most popular black restaurant was Ms. Leila Howard's Cafe. She sold the most delicious food, and she smoked a pipe and cigars."

—Louis Chestnut Jr.

This is a banquet held for teachers and their friends at the Blue Lantern in the early 1940s. The Blue Lantern opened in 1941 on the corner of South Liberty Street and Hampton and was initially operated by John Coleman and Royal Sims, two best friends. The popular nightspot was frequented by teachers and other professionals from the Southside, as well as by the soldiers stationed at Camp Croft during the early 1940s. The Blue Lantern flourished well into the early 1950s, when business slowed down and it closed. ~Courtesy, the Frank Nichols family

A banquet at the Blue Lantern during the war years, about 1942. Shep Mills is pictured at front right.
~Courtesy, Joan Mills

A boy on Clark
Alley in 1963
~Courtesy,
Elizabeth Young

(above) A cluster of houses on Elford Terrace. On the left is a house once owned by B.K. Hardin, principal of Evins Junior High School. The Joe Patton house is in the middle.
~Courtesy, Don Moss

Carrie Nell Wright Hamilton stands in front of the Collins Hotel on Liberty Street in 1968.
~Courtesy, Frances Thompson

The USO Club

A USO Club for African-American soldiers stationed at Camp Croft during World War II opened on the lower end of South Liberty Street in 1940. The USO served as a place the soldiers could read, relax, play games of shuffleboard, ping-pong, billiards, and have social functions.

At the end of the war, the building became the Liberty Street Center but was known in the neighborhood as Woodwards' Recreation Center, after the family of John W. Woodward, a local funeral director who provided financial support. Many people also continued to call it the USO years after the war ended.

Eunice Thompson, the athletic director for Highland School and a hostess for social activities for the Croft soldiers, became the first director of the center. George Long headed up activities for boys in the neighborhood. The center was used for social gatherings such as banquets, dances, and recreational activities. It was also frequented by Carver High School students, who came there daily after school, often to learn the latest dance craze. There were also piano and dance recitals (led by Addie McWhirter), operettas, and children's programs. In the early 1950s a library was put in the building. It was the first and only library that African Americans could use during segregation. Gertrude Wiggins was the librarian.

Priscilla Rumley, who ultimately became director, was hired as assistant to Mrs. Thompson by the mid-1950s. Two rooms were added, one on each side of the long porch. One served as Bennie Mansel's classroom for the black students at the Charles Lea Center. The other room was used for the teen girls' club, an important neighborhood institution headed by Mrs. Rumley. Black "candy stripers," who helped out at the "colored" hospital, were trained there also. They were taught etiquette, in addition to what was taught at home.

The old USO was a place where the R&B and gospel singers came to rehearse their acts before performing at the Memorial

Auditorium when they came to Spartanburg during segregation. By the late 1960s the center also served as a preschool day care center.

In the 1970s a new building was constructed near the Arkwright community, and the old USO was torn down to expand the Carver Junior High School campus. (The school's tennis court now sits where the USO used to be.) The center was renamed for the long-time school principal and became the C.C. Woodson Recreation Center. Priscilla Rumley was the director there until her retirement. James "Butch" Greer is the current director.

B.J. Shores drew what she remembers of the USO on South Liberty.

Collins Service Station on South Liberty
Street, looking south, in the 1940s
~Courtesy, Kitty Collins Tullis

A retail license tax stamp from
1938 for a liquor business run by
Ernest Collins, 177 W. Park Avenue
~Courtesy, Kitty Collins Tullis

Willie Mae Gilchrist inside the Southside Cafe in the late 1950s. The short order menu lists chicken, scallops, oysters, shrimp and pork shops. A T-bone steak cost $1. ~Courtesy, the Abercrombie family

(bottom left) Barber Joe D. Patton cuts the hair of Walt Brown in his shop in the basement of Bull's Clinic in May 1960. ~Courtesy, Cheryl Harleston and the City of Spartanburg

(bottom right) Joe Patton chatting with Johnny Smith at Oliver's Pharmacy in the mid-1960s. ~Courtesy, Cheryl Harleston and the City of Spartanburg

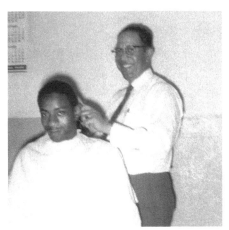

Edith Duffie visiting with cousins in Tobe Hartwell in 1942, a year after the housing project was built. ~Courtesy, Gertrude and Harry Campbell

Bea Moss and friend at Oliver's Pharmacy in August 1966 ~Courtesy, Brenda Lee and Jerry Fryer

Geneva's Cafe on Short Wofford Street, across from Little Newt's and Vi's, a popular gathering place. Many residents of the Southside patronized the black-owned businesses in this area, roughly where the Palmetto Bank headquarters and Magnolia Street Parking Garage are located today. This photograph was taken in 1957.
~Courtesy, Cheryl Harleston and the City of Spartanburg

"I was born in 1932 in a house right across from Mount Moriah Baptist Church on South Liberty Street. Rosa and Walsh Reynolds were my adopted parents. We had a big house with about eight rooms, part of which we rented to boarders. We had the restaurant called Po Boy's Lunch, and my dad worked everyday for about 40 years at the ice plant. Starting at the corner of Clement and Liberty Street, there was Abrams Funeral Home, the homes of Henry Drake, Henry Perry, and Henry Clemmons. Those were the top three bricklayers in the black community."

—James Reynolds

(courtesy, Raymond Floyd)

Collins Funeral Home, 395
South Liberty Street, as it
looked in the 1940s
~Courtesy, Kitty Collins Tullis

In later years an arch was built
over the entry gate at Collins
Funeral Home ~Courtesy, Kitty
Collins Tullis

Patricia Montgomery stands in front of the North Carolina Mutual Life Insurance building, 375 South Liberty Street, and Oliver's Pharmacy in June 1960. ~Courtesy, Barbara Collier

Lula Jeter and Ruby Jenkins stand outside the parsonage for Mount Moriah Baptist Church. ~Courtesy, Brenda Lee

Dr. J.C. Bull, barber Joe Patton, and a friend clown around outside Bull's Clinic about 1960. ~Courtesy, Cheryl Harleston and the City of Spartanburg

(above) A banquet
held at the Spartan
Star lodge in the late
1950s. ~Paris Art
Studio Photograph,
courtesy, Brenda Lee

Patricia
Montgomery,
foreground, with
Addie McWhirter,
at a piano recital at
the Recreation
Center (formerly
the USO) in 1960.
~Courtesy,
Barbara Collier

An area of Lower
Cemetery Street,
late 1960s
~Courtesy, City
of Spartanburg

(above) The B&B Insurance Agency was located in the Bull Clinic building. ~Courtesy, Odell Young

The Chestnut family home on South Liberty Street across from Carver High School. Connie Chestnut was a seamstress in the neighborhood. ~Courtesy, Louis Chestnut

"I remember Liberty Street well because we lived in the area. There was Lois Dawkins' Cafe, and next to Cromer's Store, Sis Dawkins had a cafe. I never went to the cafes but I knew what they did in there. Going up Liberty was Collins's place and there was Bull's Clinic. The ice house was next to Sis's cafe and just before you got to Collins there was Ms. Leila Howard's. Down by Mount Moriah was Prysock's shoeshine parlor. I remember all of those things, but to look at it now, you can't tell it was ever there."

—Elizabeth Young

(courtesy, Raymond Floyd)

This house, built about 1893, was one of a cluster of large residences on Elford Terrace, facing what is now East Henry Street. When it was torn down in 1973, Joe Patton, the Southside barber, lived there.
~Courtesy, Don Moss

Providence Hospital for Blacks was located on Howard Street on the north side of town. It later became Woodward Funeral Home.
~Courtesy, Cheryl Harleston and the City of Spartanburg

The building behind the abandoned service station on South Church Street was the Robin Hood Club, a popular night spot in the 1960s.
~Courtesy, Spartanburg County Regional Museum of History

This house stood on the corner of South Church and East Hampton in 1973. It was torn down shortly after this photo appeared in the Spartanburg *Journal*.

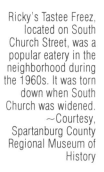

Ricky's Tastee Freez, located on South Church Street, was a popular eatery in the neighborhood during the 1960s. It was torn down when South Church was widened.
~Courtesy, Spartanburg County Regional Museum of History

The Southside Cafe as it appeared in 1958 ~Courtesy, Elizabeth Young

The Woodward Funeral Home across town on Howard Street
~Courtesy, Cheryl Harleston and the City of Spartanburg

(above) Young's Color Photography Studio was housed in the basement of the Bull Clinic. ~Courtesy, Odell Young

A "washerette" owned by James Young is flanked by Dawkins's Beer Garden, left, and Cromer's Store. This is how this section of Liberty looked in the late 1960s, just prior to urban renewal. ~Courtesy, Annie Young Gordon

Upper Cemetery Street, late 1960 ~Courtesy, City of Spartanburg

After moving to Spartanburg, James H. Young purchased property on South Liberty Street that he rented out to a laundromat, liquor store, and a church *(pictured here)*. The photo was taken a year before urban renewal came to the area. He later opened a store on Cemetery Street that operated until 1962. James H. Young Boulevard in the Tobias Booker Hartwell Campus of Learners is named in his honor. ~Courtesy, Annie Young Gordon

Cudd Street, late 1960s ~Courtesy, City of Spartanburg

"I was born June 6, 1929, in Spartanburg County. I moved to the Southside in 1955 after returning home from the Army. I remember the housing project was very nice back then because it was originally built for the service men in Camp Croft and their families, so it was built well. When I graduated high school in 1946, there were only two schools on this side of town, Carver and Carrier Street—no one on this side had to go on the other side of town to school. The kids over on Glendalyn Avenue and Ribault Street went to Dean or Cumming Street School. That area was called 'N***** Town.' I don't know why it was called that but it was."

—John Goodwin

A view down South Liberty Street, looking toward Caulder Avenue, late 1960s. The steeple of Mount Moriah Church is in the distance. ~Courtesy, City of Spartanburg

8

Residents in the Later Years

"It became clear the schools were going to be integrated and the community that we had was going to be dissipated through urban renewal and other kinds of things."

—Joe Grant

(above) "Alverta, Terry, Rosalind, Veronica and Audrey, 1965"
~Courtesy, Laura Wilson

The Chestnut family. Front: Monica and Donald; *left to right at rear:* Amanda, Louis Jr., Connie, Louis Sr., Talmadge and her husband, Dr. Bowers. ~Courtesy, Louise Chestnut

Willie Lou Mack and her scout troop in the late 1960s. ~Courtesy, Brenda Lee

The home
wedding of Ann
Lee and Second
Lieutenant Calvin
Hastie on South
Liberty Street,
May 19, 1973
~Courtesy,
Brenda Lee

(above) In this photo from the early 1960s Addie McWhirter, daughter of Mary H. Wright, stands in front of her home on South Liberty Street. Mrs. McWhirter taught music in her home. ~Courtesy, Brenda Lee

(top left) Mattie Montgomery and Lillian Allen at 148 Carrier Street in 1961 ~Courtesy, Barbara Collier

Neighborhood barber Joe Patton in his shop in the basement of Bull's Clinic. ~Courtesy, Burke Brown

Remembering the Lunch Counter Sit-in

During the 1950s and '60s, local black leaders such as the Rev. Booker T. Sears and the Rev. J. Leon Pridgeon often worked behind the scenes with white civic leaders to avoid violent situations in the civil rights struggle.

However, there were two major Spartanburg demonstrations during that era. On July 27, 1960, about 30 local African-American youths followed the example of young blacks across the South who sat down in protest at lunch counters that denied them service. In Spartanburg this was done at the Kress and Woolworth stores downtown.

Carole Moore Richard, then a teenager living at Tobe Hartwell Apartments, remembered hearing about the upcoming demonstrations from the Reverend C.M. Johnson of Majority Baptist Church. She and her sister Elaine secretly attended meetings that were designed to brief and screen potential demonstrators.

She recalled, "A burning desire to be a part of bringing about change for 'my people' and 'my community' led to my participation in the sit-ins. I have always believed in not sitting back and allowing someone else to do the work while others sit back and simply reap the rewards. We were instructed that only the spokesperson for the group would be allowed to speak. John Hilton, a former neighbor of mine, I believe was the designated spokesman. The remainder of us were to sit and look straight ahead, regardless of what transpired, unless directed by our leaders to do otherwise.

"I was anxious and scared. The fear was mostly in response to my sister's knowledge that our father had forbidden us to sit in. At the store we all entered the front door as onlookers gawked. We headed to the rear of the store where all the lunch counters were. Once there, we sat down. We were ordered to leave. There were white people standing around jeering at us. No one would serve us. After sitting there, refusing to leave, they literally roped us into the seats. I don't recall what led up to our eventually getting up to leave by the rear door, but we did. The minister who led the protest was taken to jail via the front door. As we were leaving, the white people, mostly men, spat on us and continued to jeer. One guy spat on my sister, and she kicked him. Chaos ensued, and we were running with a mob and police in pursuit."

The Spartanburg *Herald* of July 28, 1960, confirmed this account and added that a mob did, in fact, chase some of the black youth to South Liberty Street and some fighting ensued. Retired Justice Matthew Perry, who then practiced law on South Liberty Street, defended some of the African-American teenagers in court afterwards.

In 1963, one year before the Civil Rights Act outlawed segregation in public places, negotiations between black and white local leaders quietly integrated lunch counters in Spartanburg.

—Damon Fordham

This photograph of the lunch counter sit-in appeared in the Spartanburg *Herald*. ~Courtesy, Cheryl Harleston and the City of Spartanburg

Photo by B&B Studio for The Journal

Young Negroes Sit But Not Served At Woolworth Lunch Counter Here Tuesday
They Refused To Give Names; White Patrons Seemed Undisturbed As This Photo Was Taken

JUL 27 1960

Mattie Nichols was the crossing guard at Mary Wright Elementary School. She is the aunt of Frank Nichols Jr. ~Courtesy, Frank Nichols Jr.

The Nichols grandchildren at their home on Cudd Street in the 1960s ~Courtesy, Frank Nichols

Ann Nichols in the
late 1960s
~Courtesy, Frank
Nichols

Catherine Duncan, who lived on East Valley Street, was a teacher at Highland Elementary in the 1950s and '60s. She is pictured here in March 1958. ~Courtesy, Therlon Joyner

Carver High School girls Glenda Sims *(middle)* and Brenda Lee *(right)* with friend Clarice Mackabee Teamer ~Courtesy, Brenda Lee

(right) Dr. O.C. Kirkland ~Courtesy, Cheryl Harleston and the City of Spartanburg

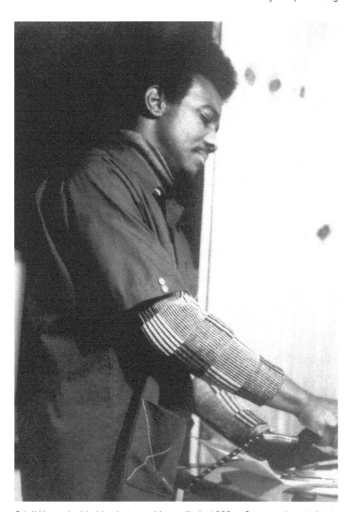

Odell Young inside his photographic studio in 1963 ~Courtesy, Loretta Nash

(right) Priscilla Rumley was one of directors of the Woodward Recreation Center, formerly known as the USO. She was instrumental in the guidance of many teenagers at the center. She led teenaged girls' clubs, which offered training in etiquette and other subjects. The Rumley Park, behind Tobe Hartwell, was named for Priscilla Rumley in 2003. ~Courtesy, Brenda Lee

« 206 »

(top left) Shepard and Bessie Richards at their home at 212 East Valley Street in 1958 ~Courtesy, Therlon Joyner

(right) Willie Duffie, mother of Edith Duffie, at her home on South Liberty Street.

(bottom left) Stella Coln at her home at 137 East Clement Street~Courtesy, Brenda Lee

(below) Thomas Young was a custodian at City Hall in 1965 when this photograph was taken. ~Courtesy, Elizabeth Young

Sisters Gail Coleman Pittard and Vicki Coleman Hogan in 1961. Their father, Emerson, was a principal at Cumming Street School and served as assistant superintendent for School District 7. Their grandmother, Katie Bethea, was a nurse at Mary H. Wright School and lived at 562 South Liberty Street. ~Courtesy, the Campbell family

Siblings Howard and Joyce Butler, dressed and ready for church on Easter morning, 1963. They are standing next to their house on Sydney Street.~Courtesy, Howard Butler

Members of the Young family. *Standing, left to right:* daughters, Brenda, Ruth, Loretta, and Johnsie; Mother, Mrs. Lillie Maude and son, Bennie; *seated, left to right:* grandchildren Dottie, Gwen, Maxine, Sandra, Terry, and Debra. ~Courtesy, Loretta Nash

Nancy Abercrombie, known as Miss Abby, at her Liberty Street restaurant in the 1950s ~Courtesy, the Abercrombie family

The Assassination of Martin Luther King Jr.

After the assassination of Martin Luther King on April 4, 1968, Spartanburg faced minor skirmishes of violence and vandalism along South Liberty Street, as opposed to the major riots that occurred in larger cities such as Detroit and Chicago. Local black ministers held a mass meeting at Majority Baptist Church, and the Reverend J. B. Glover of Trinity AME Church exhorted, "Let us both in the Southland stop blaming each other and work together. To the white man, I say respect the black man, and to the black man, I say strive to be respected." Students at Carver High School responded to Dr. King's killing by picketing the offices of the Spartanburg *Herald-Journal* for what they saw as the paper's lack of fair coverage of events in the black community, and Carver High's Black Youth Awareness Coordinating Committee picketed the local YMCA for not allowing a black youth named Willie Davis of the Spartanburg High swimming team to use its pool during the summer. One sign held by the young people read, "WE ARE HUMAN, TOO!"

—Damon Fordham

9

The Southside in Urban Renewal

ON DECEMBER 5, 1967, ROUGHLY ONE HUNDRED YEARS after Joseph M. Young and a small group of African Americans founded a community south of Main, the city of Spartanburg applied for federal funding to take the Southside neighborhood back to open land. Taking a cue from Congress and President Lyndon B. Johnson, who had declared a "war on poverty," the all-white Spartanburg City Council said it intended to relocate nearly 2,000 Southside residents into hardier housing and to build roads where new investment might flourish.

It was a painful process that would happen in some 1,400 U.S. communities—most of them African-American—across the United States from the 1950s to the 1970s. Cities like Spartanburg rushed to grab millions in urban renewal and Model Cities dollars before the political clock expired on the Democrats' "Great Society" programming. For the most part, voices that cried out for preserving history and community bonds were drowned out in those days. And in Spartanburg, where the destruction of the Southside neighborhood occurred simultaneously with federally forced integration of the schools, urban renewal was charged with an even more complex layer of emotion.

It is safe to say that none of the Southside community leaders expected the obliteration of their neighborhood, which ultimately occurred. Yet, by the mid-1960s, both blacks and whites in Spartanburg had become concerned about the deteriorating state of housing on some of the streets on the Southside. "When urban renewal came through, I thought it was a good thing for the back alley streets, because some of those houses were there long before I was born and needed to be torn down," recalled Willie B. Wilson, a long-time Cemetery Street resident born in 1922. "But I don't think they should have torn down

Warren Alley, 1966
~Courtesy,
Spartanburg Herald-Journal

Houses such as these on West Clement Alley were known as "shotgun houses" and were found in poor neighborhoods, black and white, across the South. Because no space was given to a hall, each room opened to the next, and it was said if all doors were opened at once, you could fire a shotgun completely through the house, missing the house itself. Often landlords would build as many as four on a 100-foot lot. If the house sat on a hillside, it might rest on a foundation pillar of one foot in the front and 10 feet in the back, with no underpinning to enclose the underside of the house. In the winter, the wind froze the underside of the uninsulated house as well as the sides and roof. For warmth, tenants depended on a "trash burner" stove in one room that would burn scrap wood or coal, and it was connected to the outside by a tin flu. ~Courtesy, *Spartanburg Herald-Journal*

Liberty Street, because that is where all the businesses were. When they took away Liberty Street, they messed up everything."

Housing deterioration on the Southside—indeed in many black neighborhoods in the 1960s—was part of the sad legacy of poverty resulting from decades of discrimination in education and employment. Many houses on the Southside had been built prior to indoor plumbing and sewage lines; their owners and renters, struggling to get ahead despite the lack of decent jobs, did not have the economic means to repair them or to move out. Textile jobs and mill-maintained housing were not available to the residents of the Southside, as they were to poor white families. In 1915 the South Carolina General Assembly had officially banished African Americans from the cotton mills by making segregation required by law, and that was the way it went in most large workplaces throughout much of the 20th century.

While more blacks moved into the merchant class during the boom World War II years when thousands of black Camp Croft soldiers passed through town with money in their pockets, the 1950s and '60s were tough decades for advancement. Hundreds of Southside residents remained in jobs paying just a few dollars a week; large numbers of them worked as domestics and laborers. Roughly 80 percent of

East Valley Street, late 1960s ~Courtesy, City of Spartanburg

them rented their homes. The passage of the U.S. Civil Rights Act in 1964 did not measurably improve job opportunities for blacks in Spartanburg: as late as the mid-1970s only 15 percent of the textile mill jobs in the county were held by African Americans.

Meanwhile, many landlords of Southside residents were unwilling to pay for repairs to the deteriorating homes, often blaming tenants for the constant need for maintenance. By the 1960s large numbers of houses became concentrated in a small number of hands. Some of the landlords were white, some black. One of them, R.T. "Babe" Thompson, a white man said to have owned more than 500 low-income rental houses, was a regular at Spartanburg City Council meetings where he protested newly developing public housing projects as "socialistic" and unfair competition for landlords. At one meeting he denied that there was a shortage of low-income housing in Spartanburg and complained that some people who could pay higher rents (to him) were enjoying lower rents in the housing projects. At another meeting he accused the city of failing to protect landlords through inadequate inspection and policing of rehabilitated property. As the Spartanburg *Herald* reported, Thompson had a point: the city's one inspector for rehabilitated property would have had to inspect a house every ten minutes, all year long, to keep up with the job.

Regardless, landlords like "Babe" Thompson were suspect, both in the black neighborhoods and at City Hall. The local newspaper published a story speculating that profits of substandard housing were 20 percent annually, while the landlords themselves claimed profits of only 5 to 8 percent. Although the city had passed ordinances in 1950 and 1959 requiring houses to have indoor toilets, and then hot water with either a tub or a shower, enforcement was sporadic. Fred Rigsbee of the Spartanburg *Herald* reported in 1966 about the inattention landlords were paying to these ordinances:

> Ask a tenant in such a house whether he has hot water and a tub. At first, all you get is a blank stare. ... Some tenants will say they have been promised these things "two or three years ago." But landlords forget, they say.
> Do they forget to collect (rents)? the tenants are asked.
> No they don't forget, the tenants will tell you.
> Slum housing is a gold mine, says Col. H.L. Melvin, director of city rehabilitation. This type of house brings a high return on the owner's investment: taxes are low and little if any upkeep is required. Let a piece of slum property go up for sale and everyone, it seems, is bidding on it, Melvin says.

Into this picture came urban renewal.

Because of the tight friendship of three-term Spartanburg Mayor Robert Stoddard and U.S. Sen. Strom Thurmond, Spartanburg was in the perfect position to reap a windfall of federal urban renewal dollars. Even before Stoddard took office in 1962, the first urban renewal project in the state occurred in the city of Spartanburg, in an African-American neighborhood known as Gas Bottom. So named because of its proximity to a coal-fed power plant in the area where Daniel Morgan Avenue now t-bones into North Pine Street, Gas Bottom was hardly a pleasant place to live. The plant's four smokestacks filled the air with a gas odor that lingered in the bottomland near Chinquapin Creek and Courthouse Branch. This urban renewal project was called R-1 because it was the first in South Carolina. Between 1960 and 1964, at a total cost of $900,000, 162 substandard homes were condemned and demolished in the five-square-block area of Gas Bottom and 148 were rehabilitated. About 110 families were relocated. On May 7, 1965, Spartanburg was honored for "Superior Achievement" for carrying out the urban renewal of Gas Bottom.

But Spartanburg political leaders were unhappy with a state law that prohibited them from reselling "renewed" property to a private bidder for redevelopment. As the state law stood in 1965, the land they cleared in Gas Bottom could only be used for public purposes, such as parks or public housing, and so Gas Bottom became a baseball field. Marion Bryson, the city's Director of Public Works (and the city's future Director of Urban Renewal), appeared before City Council a number of times in 1965 to argue that redevelopment would happen faster and more taxes could be paid to the city if South Carolina's constitution were changed to allow the sale of cleared property to the highest bidder.

In early 1966 State Senator Charles C. Moore of Spartanburg introduced a bill in the South Carolina Senate calling for a referendum in the November general election on the question of reselling cleared land to developers. By this time, Washington, D.C., had turned on the spigot for urban renewal dollars and had reduced the local match for federal funds from one-third to one-fourth, providing more incentive to rush for these grants. A full Spartanburg campaign to approve the constitutional amendment ensued. The *Herald*, which endorsed the proposed change, ran a series of seven articles about local housing conditions, accompanied by startling photographs of the worst dwellings in the city. Both the Chamber of Commerce and the Jaycees went on record supporting it.

The little-noticed amendment barely passed in the statewide referendum in November but drew overwhelming support in Spartanburg County. In fact, nearly half of the votes in favor of the amendment came from one South Carolina county: Spartanburg.

With that change to state law, the city of Spartanburg was off and running on its next urban renewal project—R-4, the Highlands area west of downtown. This 87-acre area was bounded by Reidville Road on the west, "Nasty Branch" creek on the east, Fairforest Park on the south, and the new Henry Street on the north (just east of where The Beacon restaurant stands today). City officials called the mostly residential Highlands area "the most blighted section of the city." At a cost of $3 million, the project demolished 286 houses and relocated 284 families, about half of them moving into a brand new 150-unit public housing unit complex on-site called Cammie Clagett Courts. (Cammie Clagett,

who lived at 723 South Liberty Street, was a long-time home economist with the Clemson Extension Service.) There was little controversy about the Highlands project reported in the newspapers. Its residents were in desperate straits, for the most part, and many seemed grateful for the opportunity to move to public housing.

Yet some controversy was already arising about the wisdom of disassembling neighborhoods, and sometimes from unexpected places. In a policy speech in Raleigh, North Carolina, before the Carolinas Council of Housing, South Carolina's 46-year-old Democratic Lieutenant Governor John C. West shocked

Urban renewal came to the Highlands area in the late 1960s. The building in the back is old Highlands School ~Courtesy, Cheryl Harleston and the City of Spartanburg

many of his colleagues back home when he charged that urban renewal had created more housing problems than it had solved. The bulldozer "has become the symbol of the type of activity which has wiped out housing units by the thousands and has not replaced them. Overlooked has been the agonizingly simple consideration of personal feelings of neighborhoods," West said in 1969. "Human beings have established roots and derive their personal identity from these surroundings." In comments published on the front page of the Spartanburg *Herald*, West called for renovation rather than demolition. Urban renewal was a short-term solution to the problem of 300,000 substandard houses in South Carolina and, he warned, public housing carried "the negative connotations of population displacement, row after row of depressingly uniform structures, what some people have called instant ghettos."

❖   ❖   ❖

As Highlands was being bulldozed, Spartanburg city officials eyed what they considered an even larger prize: the urban renewal of the Southside and federal designation as an official "Model City," which would bring Spartanburg millions of dollars for both land clearance and new social programs to help people rise from poverty.

In November 1968 Spartanburg was named one of 150 Model Cities in the nation (Rock Hill was the only other one in South Carolina). The federal program was originally conceived as a way to concentrate enough dollars to make significant social and physical changes in a few riot-torn cities such as Detroit and Philadelphia, but eventually Congress decided to spread the program over 150 cities. The grants tended to go to places where there was a powerful congressman. In Spartanburg's case, the close relationship of Senator Strom Thurmond and Mayor Bob Stoddard clinched the deal.

Thus federal funds came pouring into the city of Spartanburg—more than $8 million in 1969 alone. Model Cities became a new department at City Hall with an integrated staff described as "people helping people." They oversaw an area that was 70 percent black, 30 percent white, and they doled out large grants to public service agencies that addressed such issues as job training, child care, juvenile crime prevention, and even rodent control. Fifteen percent of the city's land mass was targeted, an area that contained roughly 20,000 people, 40 percent of the city's population.

As part of Model Cities, Spartanburg became the first city in the nation to establish what was called a "Junior Planning Staff," made up of teenagers serving as liaisons between City Hall and the neighborhoods. That initial group included black Carver High students James Cheek, Karen Moss, Patricia Boozer, and Beverly Lindsey; and white Spartan High students Robbie Deal and Ronald Jones. The group was paid to canvas the low-income neighborhoods about housing conditions, recreation needs, childcare concerns, and other issues.

The entire Southside fell under the purview of Model Cities, and many resi-

Empty homes at the corner of South Liberty and Lee streets awaiting the bulldozers of urban renewal ~Courtesy, Don Moss

dents there initially cheered its initiatives. In October 1969, the Reverend C.M. Johnson of Majority Baptist Church, vice chairman of the Model Neighborhood Authority, implored his neighborhood to "become involved."

But simultaneous with the rollout of Model Cities, plans for the razing of the Southside were gradually being revealed. Called the Cemetery Street Urban Renewal Project, or R-14, the $8 million initiative proposed to "renew" a 300-acre area bounded on the north by Irwin Street and West Park Avenue, on the east by Southern Railway, on the south by Young and Smith Streets, and on the west by North Church Street. This was to be the largest urban renewal project in South Carolina to date and included 985 residential, public, and commercial buildings. Roughly 2,000 people lived or worked there, 92 percent of them African-American.

When the federal government announced on May 13, 1969, that Spartanburg had received a $208,740 planning grant for the five-year project, the local newspaper quoted a city official as saying, "The major emphasis of the project will be on rehabilitation of existing structures."

That did not prove to be the case. Of the 909 residential dwellings in the Cemetery Street Project, initial plans called for 600 to be cleared, 110 rehabilitated, and 194 retained "without treatment." There were 76 commercial buildings, with 56 to be cleared, 7 to be rehabilitated, and 12 to be retained "without treatment." It gradually dawned on the business and religious leaders of the Southside that almost everything they valued was to be taken. (In the end, only the two public schools, Tobe Hartwell Apartments, Epiphany Episcopal Mission, and Majority Baptist Church were left standing of all the structures in the heart of South Liberty.) In July 1970 about 100 neighborhood residents packed City Council to protest the plans, to no avail.

"When urban renewal came through, Mom and Dad were living on East Valley Street, and they both regretted it," recalled Constance Manyfield. "There was nothing they could do but to find a place and move. Daddy attended the neighborhood meetings and voiced his opinions about having to lose his house. The house on East Valley Street had ten rooms and two baths—he'd done a lot in fixing up the house, like fencing around property front and back, central heat and air, and a concrete sidewalk in front of the house." Manyfield's parents left East Valley and went to nearby Alexander Avenue,

In 1966, a photographer with the *Herald-Journal* followed a city inspector on his rounds at unmaintained rental property on Cudd Street. ~Courtesy, *Spartanburg Herald-Journal*

where they stayed until they died.

To carry out the massive urban renewal undertaking, the city hired two appraisal companies to determine the value of each house before making a cash offer of purchase. They warned families to stay put until they were contacted by urban renewal officials: if they went ahead and moved, they would lose their federal relocation benefits. By law, the city was required to pay fair market value based on the condition of each house. If the property owner was not satisfied with the price, he or she could take the city to court. The law allowed an additional $5,000 in housing allowance and moving expenses for the homeowner.

For the renters, the city was required to offer "decent, safe, and sanitary housing, conveniently located, and at prices, or rents within their means." A project office, mostly to handle relocations, was set up at 205 East Hampton Avenue and operated 8 a.m. to 5 p.m. on weekdays and one night a week. Displaced families were interviewed at the office at the time of property acquisition and told of purchasing and renting options. Some of them were disappointed to find that their living costs increased as they moved to rehabilitated homes and other neighborhoods.

The first people to leave the neighborhood were moved to such public and subsidized housing complexes as Spartan Terrace Apartments, Phyllis Goins Apartments, Hub City Courts, and Woodward Homes, but it quickly became clear that Spartanburg did not have enough low-income housing. As early as 1972 the federal Department of Urban Development warned Spartanburg that up to 400 more public housing units were needed to handle the displaced families. And despite the fact that the city's 1969 application for urban renewal money had included letters from Spartanburg builders and bankers who told of their intention to construct hundreds of new low-income, single-family homes, there was no fol-

Wilma Dunlap *(right)* a social worker, interviews Mrs. Evans Bobo at her home at 544 South Liberty Street in preparation for demolition of her residence. ~Courtesy, Brenda Lee

ET HELP

INFORMATION

Urban Renewal Project Office
205 E. Hampton Ave.

Office

FROM
THIS

TO
THIS

The Urban
Renewal Project
Office was located
at 205 East
Hampton Avenue
(top).Within an
Urban Renewal
Project brochure
was this example
of replacement
housing *(bottom)*.
~Courtesy, City of
Spartanburg

In 1972 urban renewal moved Mrs. Stella Coln, grandmother of Brenda Lee, from her home at 137 Clement Street to another home at 290 Alexander Avenue. ~Courtesy, Brenda Lee

low-through on their parts. The stock of low-income houses continued to decline.

Novie Richie was in her early fifties when urban renewal happened. She and her family were living in a rental house just off South Liberty Street that was badly in need of repairs. She wished the city had forced the landlord to fix up their home, but instead their house was bought by the city and demolished. "I hated to leave there because I loved it there on Liberty Street—everything was so convenient, and right there close at hand," she recalled in an interview when she was 88 years old. "We lived across the street from the cab station, and if I had to go anywhere, I'd just go to the front porch and yell across the street, and one of them would come and get me. There were restaurants, funeral homes, grocery stores, drug stores, beauty shops, doctors' offices, and a clinic, and just about anything you wanted."

Perhaps the greatest pain for residents came when they realized that they had either misunderstood the city's real intent—or had been misled. "I thought urban renewal was a good thing, but we didn't know they were going to come through and tear down everything," Doris Stewart, a former resident of South Liberty, recalled years later. "We thought that they were going to fix up things and make it so people would have a better place to live in the same neighborhood with parks, churches, schools

A bulldozer begins destruction of a large house on South Church Street in 1973. This house stood on the current site of the Swim Center. ~Courtesy, Don Moss

Three of the large houses on South Liberty Street are pictured in the background of this photograph taken at an outdoor service of Mt. Moriah Baptist Church in the early 1970s. At the far right is a signboard erected to announce that urban renewal demolition was imminent. Left to right, these houses belonged to Dr. Walker, 546 South Liberty; William Kershaw, 544 South Liberty; and Bessie Evans, 540 South Liberty. ~Courtesy, Brenda Lee

and stores." Stewart and her family were moved to a subsidized apartment at Spartan Terrace. She now lives on White Oak Street in the Park Hills area.

Don Beatty was still a boy when urban renewal was announced, but he remembers his family thought it would improve the neighborhood. "When urban renewal came through, I thought what most of the people thought, that something good was going to happen, but all we saw was open space, once urban renewal started and stopped. There was nothing left—it was just like they came through with a bulldozer and just tore down and didn't build anything. It was devastating," said Beatty, now a South Carolina Appeals Court judge.

In September 1971, the city's urban renewal Manager Marion Bryson told City Council rather callously, "By late winter we should have some good bonfires down there." In comments reported in the local newspaper, he also added that the area "will look like a ghost town" after the razing work had been finished. Understandably, the burning of their former homes was not well received by the residents of the area. It invoked memories of cross burnings and an earlier era of violent persecution of black people in the South. Neighborhood representative Lionel L. Turner, who owned his own plumbing business, called the practice "a disgrace" and complained to the Spartanburg *Herald* that the burning of two houses on East Hampton Avenue had severely damaged three large oak trees in a site earmarked for a community park. The neighbors com-

Jessie Moore Sanders *(courtesy, Raymond Floyd)*

plained of smoke and ash, he said. "We have federal funds to hire people to tear down the houses. They should use a bulldozer or some means other than fire." Despite his complaints, the city could make him no promises. City Manager Lott T. Rodgers said burning was a good way of getting rid of snakes and rats, and besides, it gave city firefighters a place to practice their skills.

"When urban renewal came through, we were living at 192 Young Street, just a few steps from the (high) school," recalled Cora Taylor, now in her eighties. "We were renting and the landlord sold the house. Urban Renewal told us we had to move, and gave us a certain length of time to move. It wasn't long, but in that short length of time we looked everywhere." When the family couldn't find what it wanted, Cora's husband, George, who was working for a contractor, began building a house on nearby Montana Street, where Taylor has lived ever since. "When I had to leave my neighborhood, I felt like they had taken my life, and that is the worst feeling you can have, besides losing a loved one to death."

For those who didn't have to move very far, the relocation was sometimes not as traumatic. "When urban renewal came through, my parents were still living at 256 Cudd Street," said Frank Nichols Jr. "Moving was something they didn't want to do, because it was a change from the normal. They found a house on Winsmith Street which was not too far from the old neighborhood on Cudd Street, and when they found out that some of their neighbors were moving right next to them, it made the transition much smoother."

Still others saw the move as a new opportunity. Jessie Moore was living on

Young Street with her mother. "We were renting that house, so we had to move. Urban renewal was a good thing because it gave a lot of people better homes, somewhat like the ones that were on Liberty Street."

By far the greatest protests came over the clearance of South Liberty Street in front of Carver High School. Many Southside residents felt it was no coincidence that, in a year when integration brought several hundred white teenagers into their neighborhood to attend Carver (which became a junior high campus in 1970), a wide swath of land was being cleared around the school grounds. School District 7 officials said they wanted the property for recreation fields and future expansion, but Southside residents felt that they were being banished for their skin color. Black residents jammed City Hall in March 1971 to protest the removal of the houses that were not substandard. Dr. Edwin E. Oliver, the Southside pharmacist, insisted to City Council that the inclusion of the property in front of Carver High "was done out of prejudice because of the integration of the schools." Oliver speculated that replacing those comfortable homes would cost the homeowners twice what the city was paying to buy them. The city took his comments "under advisement," but urban renewal proceeded apace.

One by one, the businesses of the Southside were purchased, uprooted, or closed. Rather than find another location, many owners chose to pocket the money and not reopen their businesses. In the first wave to leave were the nightclubs and cafes: The Robin Hood Club, Ellis' Cafe, the Sportsman Club, and Hillside Cafe all departed or closed in 1971. The next year saw the purchase of Collins Funeral Home, Collins Service Station, Cromer's Grocery Store, and Mount Moriah Church. The DeLuxe Cab Company hung on until 1973, as did B & B Insurance Co., and Odell Young's Photo Studio. Among the last to go, in 1975, were the offices of doctors J.C. Bull, Vastyne Pettis, and O.C. Kirkland. Finally, in July 1975 the Southside Cafe at 505 South Liberty Street sold out, ending the parade of 85 departing businesses, churches, and professional offices. Even an eleventh-hour community plea to save the historic South Liberty Street home and schoolhouse of Mary H. Wright went unheeded.

Joe Grant, who lived in Tobe Hartwell Apartments, remembers the feeling of being disconnected from the rest of the city. "They came down Liberty Street, wiped out a lot of stuff, and started closing off the street, so we no longer had a throughway from their side of town to our side of town. The kinds of things that

The Editor:

This letter is an appeal to spare a house—a home very dear to the hearts of the daughters of the late Mrs. Mary Honor Wright, a lady honored and revered by all of us. This house is located at 400 S. Liberty Street and is to be demolished by urban renewal.

No dwelling or building in our city remains of early Black pioneers. Within the walls of this house the Mary H. Wright School was born. Within these walls, the late H.W. Ravenel, school trustee, said to Mrs. Wright, "This building is too small for so many pupils; I am going to have your school made a part of the public school system." Thus the present Mary H. Wright School had its beginning.

The writer knows nothing of architectural style save that this house exemplifies the style of an earlier period. This house could be left as an historic site for our city. It is appropriate since our nation will be celebrating our Bi-centennial. The Spartanburg Historical Society should intervene in behalf of preserving this house. Rep. Sam Manning should be alerted. The life of Mrs. Mary Honor Wright reflects dignity and service and pride upon all Spartans, white and Black equally. The Mary H. Wright School stands as a monument to her. The Mary Honor Wright Scholarship Award, the Mary H. Wright Christmas Tree keeps her memory alive and fresh and green. Even if the requirements of improving the street make it necessary that the house be moved back from the street this structure should not be razed. This house could become a museum for Black artifacts and a repository for Black culture, a place of pride and dignity for our city.

HUDSON L. BARKSDALE Sr.
Spartanburg
May, 15, 1970

from the Spartanburg *Herald*

were anti-community began happening after the urban renewal movement, Model Cities, and all of those federal programs that were supposed to improve our 'blighted neighborhood' but actually served to further isolate us from the larger world."

Ernest Collins tried to relocate his funeral home to the west side of South Church Street—where white people lived—only to run into a storm of protest about a business opening up in a residential neighborhood. After cruising through the City Planning Commission, the rezoning ran into opposition at City Council, ratcheting up the racial tension in the city. In a close vote, an angry Collins was thwarted, and his 40-year-old business was pushed farther out of the city, beyond Arkwright.

The loss of community was a constant topic of conversation. Irene Bonds, a beautician who lived on Sydney Street, remembered: "Most of the neighbors from the old neighborhood were scattered here and there, so whenever you'd run into one of them in the grocery store, there was that big familiar smile, and questions about 'where did you move to?' and 'how is the neighborhood there?' You'd just be too glad to see them."

Irene Bonds *(courtesy, Raymond Floyd)*

✧   ✧   ✧

Tainted by the outcry over the demolition of South Liberty Street, Model Cities degenerated into controversy, too. The massive program became increasingly plagued with complaints about false promises and lack of communication from City Hall. In addition, there was turmoil between white and black mem-

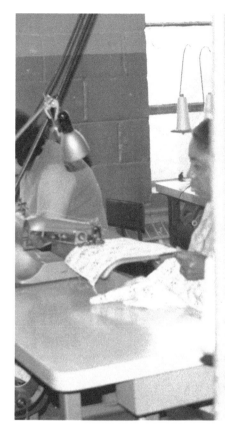
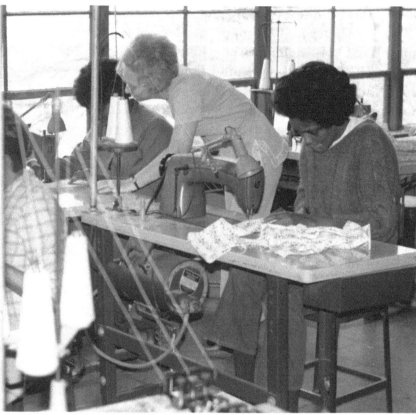

An industrial sewing class at Spartanburg Technical College was part of the Model Cities initiative.
~Courtesy, City of Spartanburg

bers of the city staff. Southside residents contacted Atlanta's Congress on Racial Equality (CORE) in mid-1970 to intervene to stop the flow of federal funds to Spartanburg until the destruction of South Liberty Street could be investigated. Their effort was unsuccessful, but federal officials did slap Spartanburg's hand in an annual program review, saying the city must address the "communication gap" with the Southside neighborhood.

Spartanburg's Model Cities Director James Thomson conceded that poor communication "between neighborhood residents and all phases of government services is one of the local program's major problems." That had "profound effects" on other individual problems, he added.

And by 1972 members of the white community began openly criticizing Model Cities, calling it "government waste." Some white City Council members and city staff members indicated they were more interested in channeling federal funds to downtown revitalization projects. President Richard Nixon and a more Republican Congress had been maneuvering for three years to pull the plug on the federal program altogether, drastically reducing Model Cities funding.

The Spartanburg *Herald-Journal*'s front-page columnist, Seymour Rosenberg, quipped in late 1972 that the demise of the federal program was imminent, and "Frankly, we think a lot of Spartans would be happy about this." That comment enraged some Southside residents who had been working hard to lift their neighbors out of poverty. Dr. J.C. Bull, the beloved Liberty Street physician, was quick to respond in a letter to the editor:

Dr. J.C. Bull was an advocate of the federal programs that brought social services to the Southside.
~Courtesy, City of Spartanburg

Perhaps there might be a lot of Spartans who would be happy about this, but I am sure that they are people like Mr. Rosenberg, who would not know that 150 poor and underprivileged children are attending Day Care because of this Model Cities Program; that a great number of their mothers are either employed or being trained for employment who were previously on welfare. I'm sure he doesn't realize, nor those other Spartans he alludes to, that projects are being implemented at Spartanburg District 7 schools, Spartanburg Junior College, Spartanburg Technical Education Center, and the University Regional Campus to help people upgrade themselves educationally and to provide opportunities for jobs, job training and skills that they would not otherwise have had without the cooperation between these institutions and the Model Cities Program.

Apparently, Mr. Rosenburg and your newspaper do not realize the role Model Cities plays in giving these people a greater opportunity to take part in the decision-making processes of the city, thereby making them better informed citizens. I would like to invite you and Mr. Rosenburg to take a tour of the Model Cities Program and projects and talk to some of the people these programs have helped to make taxpaying citizens and let them tell you if they will be happy to see this program pass …

This is a good program for Spartanburg financially and otherwise. Instead of being happy anticipating the demise of the Model Cities program, he should be asking for a city-wide Model Cities process!

Good program or not, Model Cities was history by 1973. That year Congress voted to shut off the funding valve and instead to send money to cities in Community Development Block Grants, which could be used to renovate downtowns or build parking garages as well as to address poverty issues. Hundreds of former Southside residents began adjusting to life in public housing or in different neighborhoods. Some residents found new homes on the east side of the Southside neighborhood, an area that was not cleared. Rebecca Smith, the Mary Wright School cafeteria manager, moved from her home on Park Avenue to one at 327 Alexander Street. Edith Duffie, a teacher, had owned a home on South Liberty Street since 1936. In 1974, she moved to South Converse Street. Other residents left the Southside neighborhood altogether. Carl Ellis, a coal vendor, moved to Princeton Street where he continued to ply his trade. Mary Dawkins, the daughter of businessman Roland Dawkins, moved from Celestial Street where she had lived since the 1940s, to Prospect Street. Norman and Emma Dawkins moved from Cemetery Street to Duncan Street. But many Southside residents disappeared from the city directories altogether: In some cases they were elderly people who died, but in other cases, people undoubtedly moved away in search of better opportunities and new communities.

A few houses remained on streets at the periphery of the neighborhood—Duncan, Cemetery, and Winsmith in particular—and a few longtime residents still occupied these houses. For example, Ponola Saunders, a teacher at the Mary Wright School who had lived at 143 Carrier Street since 1958, continued to reside in her longtime home in 1978. Teacher John Abercrombie (whose wife, Nancy, was the proprietor of the Southside Cafe) still lived at 141 Carrier Street that year. But his job in the neighborhood was gone: after the integration of Spartanburg's public schools, he moved from the formerly African-American Carver High School to the Daniel Morgan Vocational Center east of town.

By 1978 the area between South Church and South Liberty Streets had been mostly leveled. So were many adjacent blocks. Some streets were closed and others were re-routed as the city began the process of redeveloping the area. About 120 lucky homeowners on the eastern edge of the neighborhood

had their homes rehabilitated at no cost to themselves, but everyone else was gone. Even the formerly white-owned Victorian mansions along South Church Street, which had long-since fallen into disrepair, were gone. Mount Moriah Church moved to the corner of South Church Street and what had been formerly been Cemetery Street (now Marion Avenue). Dr. O.C. Kirkland and the Southside Cafe purchased parcels within the empty 150-acre center of the former neighborhood and started over, but no other African-American businesses were able to afford the cost of land there. A small handful of residential lots—about 30—were sold on the eastern edge of the neighborhood for new housing, but the vast majority of the area was designated for school expansion, parks, and government buildings.

(top) Julius Carson built this house in 1881 at 329 South Church Street, and this photograph dates from 1913. Carson was a druggist who later owned a small textile manufacturing plant on Crescent Avenue. This house contained Italian marble fireplaces, silver plated door knobs and a slate roof. Behind this house stood the Southside Market. The family moved out in the middle 1950s and the house fell into decline, becoming the site of a moving storage company before it was demolished in 1973 in urban renewal.

(middle) A home in the 400 block of South Church Street, torn down in 1973. "That house, in perfect shape, did not need to go," says a former resident of the area, Don Moss.

(bottom) The John Graham house, located at 354 South Church Street, built in the 1890s, now gone ~All photos courtesy, Don Moss

The opening of the Mary H. Wright Greeenway. At left is Mayor Lewis Miller. At right are Mary's family members, Bennie Mansel and Farrow Belle McWhirter. ~Courtesy, *Spartanburg Herald-Journal*

In 1978 the Southside was a gaping hole in the densely populated downtown area of Spartanburg. It had all new streets, curbs, gutters, lighting, and water and sewer lines. What it didn't have was people or connection to the past. The city and black community attempted to remedy that over the next few years by naming many of the new amenities after former residents. A park along the creek became the Mary H. Wright Greenway. A housing complex became Dr. John C. Bull Apartments; West Park Avenue became Ernest Collins Avenue. The four-lane throughway that replaced Liberty Street became Hudson Barksdale Boulevard, named for the black state legislator who got involved trying to save Mary Wright's house. A playground on the south end of the neighborhood became Patricia Rumley Park, named after the first director of the Liberty Center social services building, constructed with Model Cities money in 1970. The city sold the cemetery on Duncan Street to the Spartanburg Colored Cemetery Company, and residents, led by Farrow Belle McWhirter (Mary H. Wright's granddaughter), began a campaign to clean it up and restore it. Ultimately, a historic marker was placed there.

Government buildings gradually filled in the void. A city-owned Swim Center was built on the new Marion Avenue. Carver Junior High School picked up 35 acres for future growth. The South Carolina Vocational Rehabilitation Center went up on South Church Street, as did the South Carolina Job Service office. Mostly it was government selling to government—for the most part, the big windfall of property taxes to the city of Spartanburg did not materialize. The one bright spot was the construction in 1985 of the $5 million Heritage Court Apartments high-rise, which provided subsidized living for the elderly and handicapped.

Closer to town, the city was still busy finishing up its final urban renewal project (known as R-20 or Southside I), one of the last undertaken in South Carolina before funding ran out. This smaller redevelopment, located north of the Cemetery Street Project between Broad and Henry Streets, cleared 35 acres

Nancy Abercrombie outside the Southside Cafe after it moved to Marion Avenue during urban renewal
~Courtesy, the Abercrombie family

that held 172 homes and businesses. Ninety-five homes and businesses were rehabilitated. The city spent $5 million on R-20, and was much more successful in enticing private buyers. The area filled in with mostly white lawyers' and physicians' offices, retail stores, and a bank. All told, the two urban renewal projects had cleared some 40 city blocks.

For those who moved to public housing, the next decade often brought warmer winters and cooler summers but more deterioration in housing conditions and plenty of crime. Tenants complained that the government-owned housing was rat and roach ridden—hardly an improvement over the homes they were moved from. By 1980, the shortage of public housing was called "chronic" by one city official, and the vacancy rate was the second lowest in the state, meaning the waiting list was hundreds of names long. No new units had been built since 1975. Tenants at Tobe Hartwell complained about leaks and standing water on porches and sidewalks.

Another decade passed, and public housing in Spartanburg was in a state of crisis. Fully 20 percent of the city's residents were living in some kind of subsidized housing—8,000 people in 16 complexes—and many were unhappy, complaining of bug infestations, dark streets, and dangerous playgrounds. The drumbeat for the firing of long-time Spartanburg Housing Authority Director Frank Gooch began in 1989, with the League of Women Voters and the NAACP leading the charge. Roy Henderson, the only black member of the Housing Authority board, resigned from the agency's five-member governing panel, comparing its workings to South African white rule. Citizens charged the agency with hoarding grant money that could have been used for social service programs, such as job training and homework centers. Eugene Goodwin, the on-site manager of Tobe Hartwell, spoke out at City Council about rats, holes in apartment walls, and appliance problems; the Housing Authority promptly demoted him and docked him $6,000 in pay. (City Council later restored his position and pay.)

In 1992 Frank Gooch retired after 33 years, and an era of reform in public housing began. Four years later, the Housing and Urban Development Department declared Tobe Hartwell distressed and obsolete; it was torn down and replaced with the upscale, $15 million Tobe Hartwell Community of Learners neighborhood of detached housing.

As the 21st century dawned, one of the last Southside landmarks, the former

Carver High School, built in 1938 to serve the black teenagers of the city, came down and was replaced by a new, more modern junior high school. The loss of the original Carver building was a bittersweet moment for two generations of African Americans who had studied in its classrooms and competed on its sports teams. The 50-year-old Mary H. Wright Elementary School was closed, too, and a new building was constructed adjacent to Carver. Majority Baptist Church decided to upgrade its facilities and tore down the old church to make way for a larger church in 1998.

In 2005, only tiny Epiphany Mission, where Mary H. Wright and her sister Clara Young taught lessons from the Bible almost 100 years earlier, remained standing. A relic from a time long past, Epiphany, with its steeply pitched roof and dark red siding, remains at 121 Ernest Collins Avenue, tucked in between parking lots and newer Baptist churches. It stands alone as a testament to the thousands of black Spartans who had lived and worked on a street called Liberty.

◇ *Researched and written by—*
* *The Hub City Writers Project: Betsy Teter, Nancy Moore, Melissa Walker, Beatrice Hill, and Brenda Lee*
* *Melissa Walker's fall 2004 African-American history class at Converse College: Kim Anderson, Jeff Callis, Michael Colebank, Heather Couch, Sheila Davis, Amy Driggers, David Eaton, Jennifer Gray, Angela Haney, David Kelly, Douglas King, Libby Long, Elizabeth Ann Moore, Katherine Morrison, Kimberly Newton, Merry Poore, Elizabeth Sloughter, Traci Taylor and Michael Tumblin.*

This photograph of Dr. Edwin Oliver was taken after his popular pharmacy moved to Baltimore Street in the 1970s. The pharmacy was originally located at 375 South Liberty Street and was torn down for urban renewal. ~Courtesy, City of Spartanburg

⟡10

Memories from Urban Renewal

*"I don't think we knew the harm
we did emotionally to our people.
I know progress has its price, but
that is a price I think we could
have done a little bit better job
of and not have allowed it to be
as harsh as it was."*

—The Reverend Benjamin D. Snoddy

(courtesy, Raymond Floyd)

Charles Atchison Sr.

Charles Atchison, president and owner of Atchison Chartered Services, started out on the Southside in a business on South Liberty Street. Charles grew up in Tobe Hartwell, attended Foster's Chapel for elementary school, and was a member of the 1946 graduating class of Carver High School.

When urban renewal came through here, we were living on Caulder Circle. At that time we owned a business on Liberty Street across from Bull's Clinic. We moved there from Cumming Street in the '50s. We were on Liberty Street quite a few years before urban renewal came through, and I owned the property next door to the cab lot and a few other homes around the area. Urban renewal was good and bad, good for some and bad for others.

If you actually owned the property and had good records, you could do well with urban renewal, but if you didn't have and didn't keep good records, urban renewal was not a good thing. Back in those days the mom-and-pop stores kept their money in a cigar box, and at the end of the day they'd take it out and put it in the bank. They didn't keep any records of what was sold or how much was sold. Truthfully, mom-and-pop stores hardly paid any taxes. You'd go do what you wanted to do and nobody bothered you much back then.

It was for that reason that they didn't have any permanent records, and they didn't have anything to show. Urban renewal was a good project, and they had their guidelines. If you had a value of "x" amount of dollars invested, then you were able to get a value of "x" dollars back. But if you didn't have any value or couldn't show any profit or loss statements for the past three years, then you couldn't get anything.

The ones that didn't have any records or couldn't prove anything got an automatic $5,000 for going out of business, or something of that nature, and that was all they got. As far as moving, urban renewal didn't bother my business, clientele-wise, because I'd experienced it. At that time there were two things going on: there was urban renewal and the uptown development. I had just purchased the Yellow Cab Company on Dunbar Street downtown. We moved from one part of Liberty Street to the upper part, across from the Dixie Damp Laundry.

Spartanburg wanted to do the water tower project so I had to move again, and I had moving expenses, since I'd paid a good price for that property. I sold it to the city for a good price, so it worked out fine for me. The other businesses on South Liberty Street—some did well, and some didn't. ... But a lot of them did not do well. If they owned, they got a fair market appraisal, and some relocated to other locations, and some just closed their doors. There were a lot of mom-and-pop stores on South Liberty Street and when urban renewal came through, they closed down. Overall, I think if the people in that area had someone to tell them or to have shown them what and how to do things, then they would have fared better than they did. The major issue was having permanent records, [showing that you had paid] your taxes, because when the time comes, and you need them, and you don't have them, then you lose.

—Interview by Beatrice Hill

Norman Dawkins

(courtesy, Raymond Floyd)

Norman Dawkins was born in 1943, grew up in the Cemetery and Duncan streets area, and was a 1961 Carver graduate. He is currently serving as owner and operator of the Community Mortuary.

I was born in Hendersonville, North Carolina, but moved back to Lake City when I was a year old. We are known as Geechies. I discovered most recently that Geechies are like Africans—we all speak in the present tense. I attended first and second grade in Lake City, and when I started third grade, my teacher, Mrs. McNair (mother of Ron McNair, the astronaut) moved me up a grade, thinking I'd be put back when coming to Spartanburg, and to avoid that she promoted me to the fourth grade (in those days if you transferred from a county school to a city school, you were put back a grade), but I wasn't put back when I arrived in Spartanburg.

My dad moved me to Spartanburg in 1951 due to a severe asthma condition. Having skipped the third grade, my fourth grade teacher at Mary H. Wright placed me in a seat next to Willie Beatty, who I think is a brilliant person because he helped me to adjust to the new school setting, which worked out well. I also attended and graduated from Carver High School. To me, Carver was like the Booker T. Washington philosophy, gearing blacks for trades like carpentry, mechanics for the boys, and home economics for the girls, to become servants in the homes of others. I don't feel like enough was expected of us then.

When you look back to 400 years ago, and to [the problems that] blacks have today, it is due to what happened in the past. There are people who want to conveniently say, "We weren't responsible for slavery, it was our ancestors, we don't do those things." Well, they didn't do it themselves, but they are the ones benefiting and profiting today from the labor of our ancestors, so they are very much a part of it. I don't separate it. It's one continuum in the same sense that we as black folk continue to experience residue of slavery, and all that followed it.

When we talk about the Southside and look at our history as a whole, we know that the Southside grew out of a period of segregation. We had from 1915 to 1965 a period where blacks had their own economy—small businesses, services, and people felt themselves as part of a whole economy. What happened in 1965 was another form of disenfranchisement of black people. This didn't only happen in Spartanburg, it happened everywhere, because each little town had the black small businesses, doctors, dentist, and service stations.

Under the guise of urban renewal [some people] effectively put the blacks out of business. Some of us saw what was happening, and many of us, either didn't see, or refuse to see it for what it was, because out of fear and traditional intimidation what we know as law and authority is ultimately nothing but the power of force that could be called upon to enforce and impose the will of white folk. The reason for that is there were too many ministers, business and professional people, who all around the country, were raising issues of civil rights. They were the only ones who could afford to, with the support of the community.

To my knowledge, I don't know of any protesting of any substance in Spartanburg, until it was too late. There was an atmosphere of fear in the black community, and they had reason to be, because in the past, as black folk, they had been bombed, shot, killed and lynched, through out the years. We as a people have been terrorized in America. Law and order has always meant suppression and exploitation of black people. It is important that we recognize that the same people who wrote the Declaration of Independence were slave owners, and to them black people were not regarded as human beings.

The small businesspeople on the Southside often extended credit to people, and when urban renewal came through, they found it cost-prohibitive, with all the paperwork involved in moving and relocating. My father, who like many others and after all the years of building his business and to have it taken away without any regards, literally died from heartbreak because they couldn't compete with the larger businesses, buying and selling products at a cheaper price.

What happened on the Southside was by design. It didn't happen overnight. It had been planned with a purpose in mind, and they pretty well accomplished it. Homes that were livable were destroyed, and people had to go in debt again. Urban renewal tore down the community, section by section, much of which could have been refurbished or restored, that took away the support base of the community. When we look at South of Main, we should see that Main Street is still there, and so is south of Main Street, but what happened to it? And why? Most importantly, where do we go from here?

—Interview by Beatrice Hill

Dewey Tullis

As black businessmen in the area, we decided that we wanted to get rid of the slum area, clean it up. The group of us said, "Let's improve our neighborhood." They made it be known to the mayor and his people that we wanted to get rid of the slum area. There was a lot of money available in the government for this type of thing. We did not know that when they said "urban renewal" that they were going to take the entire neighborhood. We didn't read far enough into the plans, and we did not know how to go and ask somebody who knew about plans like that.

We were so intent on getting rid of the slum area and building something better for the people there, or at least have it so that we could build something better. We did not know that urban renewal meant removing our black businesses. … When you got paid on Friday or Saturday, the money was mostly circulated within the neighborhood, the money stayed there.

There was no representation for the neighborhood. We had no blacks on the city council or in the city government. The blacks who did have jobs there were in no position to help. If you had a problem, all they could do was to refer your problem to somebody else before anything could be done. Our main focus was to get rid of only the slum area, not Liberty Street. Hudson Barksdale Boulevard wasn't even on the original map. In the beginning we actually took a pen and drew the road plans ourselves. We wanted Liberty Street back on the map so we drew a road from Caulder Avenue to East Lee Street.

When they said it was going to be necessary for them to wipe out Liberty Street, we immediately called in a man from New York, a consultant to meet with the black business leaders. The development of a strip mall was considered, and only two men from that group of business people agreed to support and finance it. Those men were John Woodward and E.L. Collins. The other businessmen and women from that area decided they were going to sell out, take the money, and build elsewhere, and that is what happened.

We did not know that in order to stay in the area close to the people, Mount Moriah Baptist Church was [going to have to be] forced to move to a spot where it is landlocked, with almost no room to expand due to being surrounded by non-profiting, city-owned property. We didn't know there would be a nursing home in the middle of what used to be Liberty Street. I don't think we understood what we had in Liberty Street, and now we wish we had it back.

—Interview by Beatrice Hill and Brenda Lee

The Reverend
Benjamin D. Snoddy

(courtesy, Raymond Floyd)

The Reverend Dr. Ben Snoddy arrived in Spartanburg in 1976 as senior pastor of Mount Moriah Baptist Church, as urban renewal was wrapping up on South Liberty Street in Spartanburg. He is currently serving his 30th year as senior pastor of the church.

I became the pastor of Mount Moriah Baptist Church, which was at 547 South Liberty Street, in 1975, and I moved to Spartanburg in January of 1976. The original parsonage had been destroyed at that time, and the only buildings I remember still existing in the immediate area at that point were the Dawkins Smith Funeral Home, the Southside Cafe, and Dr. Kirkland's office. Those buildings were not occupied and were torn down shortly after my arrival.

The negotiations for the church property had taken place prior to my arrival. I do know that Mount Moriah was paying $300 a month for rental of the property because it had already been sold, and they were paying rent to stay there. The city was pressuring Mount Moriah to move because the original evacuation deadline had passed. They had purchased a lot where the current Mount Moriah stands today, with a parking lot in the back. The church did not have the collections of bigger funds financially to build and were not raising a lot of money at that time. There was not a surplus of money, with the exception of the money made from the selling of the old property.

About a year after I came to Mount Moriah, I learned that the same thing was happening in Nashville, Tennessee. Whoever was in charge of that project had in the guidelines that any institution that was going to add to the long life of the redevelopment of that community could get property for one dollar, and that church bought their property for one dollar when they gave up their old property. There was nothing or anything of this sort ever offered to Mount Moriah, not even a small percentage off.

When we started the building we're currently in, it was to be for 1,000 people. The city told us that we couldn't [do that] due to the guidelines in the city ordinances in reference to adequate parking spaces. By the time we started to build the new addition (The Family Life Center) we were up against the same thing, but this time we had the knowledge of professionals who looked into another ordinance committee that provided variances, which allowed us to use the parking facilities of buildings across the street for additional parking if needed. No one told us about this before.

Mount Moriah did not get property of fair and equitable value in exchange for the property of the old church that was given up. There was no kind of deal in place that many of the churches across the country got. I think that probably the churches that did get a good deal were churches who were politically positioned with the proper political leaders and city leaders—in other words, the "we'll help you now, and you can help us later" attitude. Those were the churches who got the best deals and also the churches who were knowledgeable about urban renewal, the ones that really knew for themselves what it was all about and didn't have to take someone's word for it.

Those churches had either a senator and/or representation from the U.S. Congress that belonged to that church. They had somebody in place who knew and understood what the laws of urban renewal said, and they were in a position to raise questions about things, and were able to get a better equitability. I think the whole urban renewal project, country-wide, was designed to dilute the voting power and economical power in the black communities because we lost a lot of entrepreneurs and businesses.

I didn't live in Spartanburg at the time, but I remember from just passing through Liberty Street, there were restaurants, cafes, cab stations—and some undesirables, but at least someone was making a living. Now, to buy anything except gasoline, beer, and Chinese food, you'd have to go to the other side of town. When I first came to Spartanburg, one of the things I constantly heard and read in the newspaper were the promises that urban renewal was going to come through and put back the homes and businesses into the community, Now where are they? I don't see it.

Since I've been at Mount Moriah, I have visited a lot of older members who had been relocated due to urban renewal, and I listened, and saw how they grieved so much—about how they had worked for 30 or so years, and paid for their homes, then not getting the valued dollar for the house they deserved. They were forced to move into houses that had extensive electrical, plumbing, and repair problems that they could not afford to pay for, because all of these years, they had worked to pay their home off, and were looking forward to retirement. Those are the people who went into emotional depression and some literally died of depression.

The older people really opened their hearts and talked to me about how urban renewal literally took their homes and gave them little or nothing for it. What they offered may have in some ways been better than what they had, but the people couldn't afford it. Some received monthly checks that could barely cover a monthly house payment, but no funds were left for the upkeep, like repairs, painting, etc.

I don't think we knew the harm we did emotionally to our people. I know progress has its price, but that is a price I think we could have done a little bit better job of and not have allowed it to be as harsh as it was. I think the church served as a place of healing for the community, during and after the loss of the community, because all of the members who lived in the community still came to church, including the ones that moved out quite a distance. The church played an important and needed part in the comforting and healing of the community.

—Interview by Beatrice Hill and Brenda Lee

James Talley

On the Southside there was no disconnection between church, school, and community. I think when we saw the idea of urban renewal coming, we thought it would enhance that lifestyle. We didn't know it would destroy it. It was called urban renewal, but the renewal part never took place. In my estimation there were some communities that benefited from it, but the Southside was not one of those communities. Back of the college (behind Wofford College) was not one of those that benefited, even though there were some new structures built in those areas. Highland had Cammie Clagett Apartments to come in, and that gave them a better life in housing than they had there, but it also created a little bit of disappointment because there were businesses lost there also. All of that was centered around what was happening on the Southside or the "Baptistside" of town. We had the churches, the businesses, we had the structure of building a small south-side town, so when you had that structure there, it was organized.

I think everyone there knew there had to be a change there, but no one expected it to be so drastic, to the point of losing it all but the memory. The toughest part about it is, with the exception of the Church of Epiphany, there is not a single sign or symbol of any of those things that were there. It's all in memory. Unless we do what we haven't done in the past and record it somewhere with both pictures that we find and the words that are used from some of us who are 60 years old or better, then our children will not know that the struggle was hard. The struggle was what made us what we are today; if we are anything, it was due to the struggle.

When urban renewal came through, I was in college at Livingstone. The concept was good in a sense that we were going to remove all of the pre-war, dilapidated houses, and we were going to rebuild—that was what we were told, or that was how it was presented, as a new era. [People] were told that a new Model Cities neighborhood was coming, which sounded good, because all those houses where you could look through the floor and see the ground, look through the ceiling and see the sky, winter wind coming through the walls like the door was open, were coming down. Everyone was looking forward to this new Model Cities neighborhood.

What the people didn't see was that all this property was being bought with the promise that they could buy it back once it was cleared off, but nobody thought the price would quadruple. Nobody thought to say or ask, "How are we going to buy it back?" Now that we are smarter and have been in that type of negotiations, we know; but then, we didn't know. We were looking for that end of the rainbow. When we look back now, we think, how did we miss that? But we just didn't know, and we can't blame anyone, because we just didn't know.

There were a few of us who saw it, and were able to take advantage of some of the things that were happening then, but the masses of us didn't see it. Most of us at that time who lived in those pre-war, dilapidated houses didn't own a lot of property. We didn't have the capital to buy a lot of property, if any at all. In fact, very few owned their homes. You may have found a few that owned their homes, and if you went down Liberty Street, you'd find a few more that owned their homes—because Liberty Street was the Southside's Main Street, and the people who owned businesses owned their homes also—but the masses of us rented.

Not near as many people were able to get better jobs because of education. A lot of people went up North or out West to other states looking for better-paying jobs, while their parents, in a rented house, labored and stayed here. A few came back and bought homes for their parents, but most of them didn't. There were a lot of parents who had those 15- or 25-cent insurance policies—the insurance man would come to the house, collect the money, and mark the policy paid for that week. They paid on those policies for years, and when they died, you'd find it was only worth two to three hundred dollars. It was that type of thing, urban renewal was like a bad insurance policy—sounded good from the beginning, the words were good, but when it was time to pay off, they couldn't produce.

—Interview by Beatrice Hill and Brenda Lee

(courtesy, Raymond Floyd)

Richard B. Wheeler Sr.

Richard Wheeler was born on the Southside in 1944, lived on Cemetery Street, and attended Carrier Street School just before it was torn down. Some of his fondest memories of growing up as a child were "playing with my friends, attending church, and doing other types of recreational activities, and going on outings with my family." He retired as an administrator for the District 3 school system. He is married to Sarah Wheeler and they have a son, Richard Bernard Wheeler Jr. Here he reflects on his neighborhood's difficulty in recovering from urban renewal.

When urban renewal started, we were living at 133 Cemetery Street, and we were caught up in the urban renewal process. At the time urban renewal came through I had left home for college and returned and was teaching at Highland Elementary, so basically I was living across town. But my parents were still in the home place at 133 Cemetery Street, and upon urban renewal they moved to 118 Harvard Drive. My parents realized that moving was something they had to do as a part of the urban renewal process. They wanted to be cooperative [so] that they would receive a substantial house that would equal the exchange from the home they would be giving up on Cemetery Street.

I feel the urban renewal program was intended, from what I understand, to come through and revitalize the neighborhood—to replace homes, but also to put back into the community. A number of businesses have been replaced, and a number of homes have been replaced on the Southside, but very little of that displacement has been restored. I understand that there were store venues that were supposed to have been a part of the urban renewal process on redeveloping the Southside.

After the people were initially displaced, it was just left undone. I think to appease the people, some streets were named after well known people like Hudson Barksdale, and a park was put there; but for the most part the Southside community as we knew it, starting at West Park Avenue, just vanished.

What happened in urban renewal is that the "neighbor" was taken away from the neighborhood, and what was left was the "hood." What we have to do now is to put the neighbor back into the neighborhood and lift up our people. In order to bridge the gap between the black and white people, and since we now have representation in the City Hall, we need to go back to the table with our city leaders. When we are there, say to them, "Here are some things that still need to be done many years after urban renewal."

We want to know what we can do to help these things come to pass, because we too want the best for our community; We want to live out the dream that urban renewal was really supposed to be about from its early existence—not to blame any particular group now for the [failures] of those persons who did not follow through with all of the recommendations that were supposed to have been carried through at the time of urban renewal.

I think our people will have to become more involved, more vocal, and become well-read in terms of what the real issues are. To be willing to vote and let those people who are in position to make decisions know that we need to be given favorable considerations or we will just look at voting them out of office, and placing someone else there who can get the job done. No one else can help us, like we can help us, but we cannot sit idly by and wait for someone to give us our turn. We have to help ourselves.

It's important that we have a well-documented history of the Southside, to show that we had neighborhoods that were tied closely together. They may not have compared from a financial standpoint with other communities, but to help bring back the black pride that we once had. Then we can begin to make progress again. I think it's important for people to become more caring, one for the other, that is your blessing, and as you share and help each other, it will come back to you. I think the initial spirit of urban renewal was good, but I'm not so sure as to whether it was as effective as the original intent.

—Interview by Beatrice Hill

(courtesy, Raymond Floyd)

Kitty Collins Tullis

I remember my dad had a friend by the name of Weaver, who was in charge of the urban renewal in Washington, D.C., and he went there to help get the money in here. They both belonged to the Omega fraternity and had been friends for years, but things didn't go like the black people thought it would go. Urban renewal displaced black businesses, doctors, dentists, black everything. In my neighborhood there were teachers, doctors, lawyers, and business people—they lived there, and they had businesses around in that area.

When urban renewal came through, they were telling you about this and that, and they didn't give you that much for your stuff anyway. You almost had to start all over again. We bought the house where my sister lives on [the west side of] Hampton

« 255 »

Avenue, thinking we were going to move the funeral home there. So when the [white] people in the Hampton Heights neighborhood realized that we were buying the house, they tried to block it, but my dad paid cash for it and they couldn't block that, but they did block the funeral home from being there [using zoning regulations].

We went farther down on South Church Street and bought another place for the funeral home. The service station and the liquor store we moved to the corner of Milster and Church streets after we bought that little place there. Before we bought that place, it belonged to Sellers Fish Market, and they didn't want to sell to us, so when they found out that blacks had bought it, [someone] went in and tore the building up, but then they had to go back in and fix it up again because my dad sued them. After a while, we later rented it out to the barbershop.

My dad never financed anything; he always bought it straight out. At first we were the only blacks who owned any property on Church Street. Then we tried to get the Spur station, but that man wanted to lease it out and my dad didn't want that. Urban renewal tore up the businesses, the neighborhood, they moved you from the neighborhood, and they called themselves integrating the businesses, but the white folk are the ones who had the businesses.

After urban renewal, the only people who could really hang on were the people who had a little money, but those who were just doing day-to-day were wiped out. The only things that really survived were the taxi cabs, the funeral homes—and the service station survived because you'd give credit to the professionals and they would pay once a month, and the doctors did the same thing. Those who didn't have any money, things went downhill for them.

Urban renewal moved people over a couple of streets—Union, Converse, streets like that, and parts of Duncan Park, the parts where the lower white class lived—but the blacks never did get into the big houses. I remember we were going to buy [a] home there on Union Street and we had gone through the whole process, and when [the owner] found out that Ernest Collins was black, she took the house off the market. I think later some other white family bought it, and I don't know who has it now.

—Interview by Beatrice Hill and Brenda Lee

Fannie Richie

Once while we were still living on Liberty Street, some men came through with a questionnaire and a portable model of a city. They asked us, if we had a choice and they were building a "model city," what would we like to put in it? And we of course answered with the usual: churches, schools, grocery stores, hotels, drugstores, etc., almost all of the things we presently had on Liberty Street. When Model Cities didn't happen in this area, they built Lake View Manor, which was poorly-built, prefab homes that left the people who bought there in regret. That was their "model" neighborhood.

Liberty Street was a place where everybody cared about each other, a roosting place. It was home. A lot of businesses didn't want to move but some sold out and didn't restart, and the ones that did relocate lost a lot of their clienteles and never recouped. There were times whenever there was an affair at the church, or graduation at the auditorium, practically the whole neighborhood was there. This meant a lot to the children because they knew we cared. It's not the same anymore.

I heard at one point when integration started in the schools, the people in Duncan Park (which was all white at that time) did not want their children coming through a predominantly black neighborhood to get to Carver. This was one of the reasons they came up with the Model Cities. We didn't have any representation so we didn't know what was going on, or why? Our people did not know about those things. You'd hear bit and pieces about it, but nothing concrete. So this is why [the whites] turned it around—so they wouldn't have [black neighborhoods] to go through.

There was [white] Jenkins Junior High up on North Church Street where the Spartanburg Housing Authority is now, and Carver High down on the lower part of South Liberty Street. Jenkins would get out at about ten minutes before Carver did so there would be no intermingling, because most of them lived in that area. We used to vote at Jenkins before it was torn down. I don't know what happened, but after Model Cities came through, the people got all scattered, and you would be living around the corner from people you grew up with and not know it, where in the old neighborhood, you knew everyone.

I remember during the summer months we'd hear the teenage boys on the street corner, singing "Doo Wop" songs, harmonizing at night, nobody bothered them. My aunt cooked at the W & W cafeteria, and my friends and I would go and walk home with her when she got off, coming through the white part of Liberty at night, safe, because nobody bothered anybody.

Nowadays, you see people here from other countries, and they bring their cultures with them. The South Liberty Street community was our culture, our history, and they took it all away. I think our culture was destroyed and we are trying to go back and recapture, but it's hard to recapture what is lost. I hope this book is a success and an inspiration to the young people, letting them know that if they become complacent about things, it can be taken away.

—Interview by Beatrice Hill and Brenda Lee

James Cheek

(courtesy, Raymond Floyd)

James Cheek grew up in the Phyllis Goins and Woodview areas during the 1950s and '60s and graduated from Carver High School and Wofford College. He was a teenager when urban renewal and Model Cities came to the Southside. He is now a practicing attorney in the city of Spartanburg.

There was an advertisement for Model Cities that came through the school when I was a senior at Carver High. I was hired as a junior executive, along with three other black and two white students. We went through some training, and our job was to go out and survey the community and make suggestions to enhance what was there. We started with [suggesting] improving the parks. We wanted little incubators of businesses back then, but a lot of the ideas were not followed through.

We went door to door doing surveys, trying to find the weak areas in the community and what would it take to enhance them. Now that I look back, I think we were used. I don't think Model Cities ever intended to take all those ideas of improving the community seriously. I think their intent from the beginning was to destroy.

The blacks were told they had to move out of the community. No one explained to them there was money to go into the community and renovate those houses, redo the streets, sidewalks. There were lovely tree-lined avenues there. Just off the streets were alleys—no one explained to them that bathrooms and other things could be put in most of those houses to bring them up to standard. We never surveyed the community to share that type of information. The information we were instructed to give out was all about what was wrong with the community and never what was right with our community.

I don't think the questions were drafted and drawn to elicit responses of pride, but instead to make the people think that what we had was substandard and that it had to go. I believe there were people who [became wealthy] off of the inside information that they had. ... These are the people who went into real estate and construction because of the inside information they had, because they knew the money was there. They bought those houses for little or nothing, sold them, and they benefited from the funds that should have gone directly to the homeowners, and to repair the substandard homes to bring them up to standard.

The people who were displaced were pushed pretty much into one or two areas, the Converse street area for some, and the whites from that area bought new homes. Those are the homeowners and the realtors who benefited, and the other people who were displaced had to take what they could get.

It was highway robbery—it had to be in violation of federal laws, and it was an American tragedy. We [gave up] ownership, independence, and pride. Largely, the people who got displaced never got a community they could have control over, and enhance, because it took all of their money to maintain those houses they got and couldn't bring them up to the standard of showplaces. The homes on South Liberty Street were showplaces, and some were built about the same time as the ones in Hampton Heights.

Some of the buildings on South Liberty Street were taken by eminent domain—and that is where the city can establish a "high purpose," and they can do that, but I think the "high purpose" then was to level that community. I think it was more than the buildings—it was that sense of black independence. A number of black businesses were there, and the only way to destroy it was to level it.

In Model Cities we started out in an office in the City Hall, but there was a lot of displeasure by other whites back then to have that number of blacks in and out of any office in the City Hall. So they moved us out of there into this horrible old building. All of the decisions for Model Cities were made by an all-white city council, and there were no blacks on city councils then. There's no justification for what happened in Spartanburg through Model

Cities on South Liberty Street, and there is nothing to show for it. What happened to the money?

I think there was a lot of effort made to just disperse the black community, tear it apart, and they were largely successful in doing so. I don't know of any one area where we have more than two or three businesses adjoining each other [now]. That strength is gone, and we've suffered for years because of it. Dawkins Smith Mortuary, O.B. Gray contractors, Dr. Bull's clinic, Ernest Collins' hotel, barbershops, restaurants—all of those businesses were right there together. They could have held a black Chamber of Commerce meeting right there with a ten-minute notice. Now, they've been dispersed all over the county and we can never generate that again. I think they found a way of destroying that and used federal funds to do it with. There ought to be an investigation made to find out what happened, and I think Congress ought to be held accountable, even now, because if it happened in Spartanburg, it happened other places also.

—*Interview by Beatrice Hill and Brenda Lee*

Brenda G. Lee

Brenda Lee was born in a boarding house on South Liberty Street and moved to Tobe Hartwell with her family when she was very young. She became the first African-American female legislator in Spartanburg County in 1995 and served in House District 31 in the South Carolina House of Representatives for ten years.

The big news came about us having to move from South Liberty Street. I was living with my parents, James and Costella Foster. When the city representatives would come to see us, they never had all the information. One day we were told that we'd have to find a place to rent. Then the next time somebody would come back and say that we could buy. My parents were very upset about having to move because my sister was at South Carolina State, and they were concerned how they were going to pay her tuition.

When we found a house to move in, my dad used his VA loan to secure it. When I think back on the whole transition, I'm not convinced that anyone was looking out for the best interests of my parents or my grandmother, who also had to leave her house on Clement Street. I don't know that they had all of the knowledge they needed to make the right transaction as far as real estate is concerned.

My grandmother lived alone and she handled those transactions herself. The house my parents moved into at 291 Alexander had many flaws—this was their first experience in buying a home, and they didn't know what to look for, and no one told them. My grandmother bought the house across the street from my mother, and she always had problems with her roof leaking and plumbing problems. I remember her saying that when she first bought the house, there was a big chandelier in the living room and when she returned with her furniture, the chandelier was gone. Little things like that made me believe that a whole lot of things went on in that whole transaction where people were taken advantage of. I believe my grandmother was taken advantage of when she was sold that shell of a house—supposedly when you moved from one area to another through urban renewal, you were suppose to have the electrical and plumbing all in place.

When we started this book project, I got a chance to look through the 1970 city grant that started all this urban renewal. For the masses of the people who probably wanted to become homeowners, there was no program in place to help them. They were moved from one environment of paying rent to another environment of paying rent. The ones who benefited from the overall project were the large landowners who owned land on the Southside. As I looked through the report, the majority of those people were white people, and only a few non-whites who were businessmen. The grant said there was going to be a shopping area on Barksdale Boulevard, and that never happened. They had reports from realtors—one said he was going to build 100 low-income houses in three years; another said 125 houses in three years. I haven't seen that happen either.

Urban renewal was a very sad time for me, and it hurts my heart when I think of the momentum we lost as a community. If we still had that momentum today, it would be a totally different situation in Spartanburg, as far as economic development and families are concerned in the black community. I don't think the families who were displaced from the Southside were top priority in that whole movement. I really think it was about something else, with very little emphasis being placed on the families. There were millions of dollars spent for that Cemetery Street Project, and the percentage that went to help and to relocate families, and to help them stay together was not there. They were dispersed throughout the community, and they were totally away from their political base, totally away from the areas that they were familiar with.

That was the past, but we have to be careful to think first when we start to talk about tearing down communities and displacing people, because of the pain it causes. I've stayed here because this is my home, my heritage and I love this community.

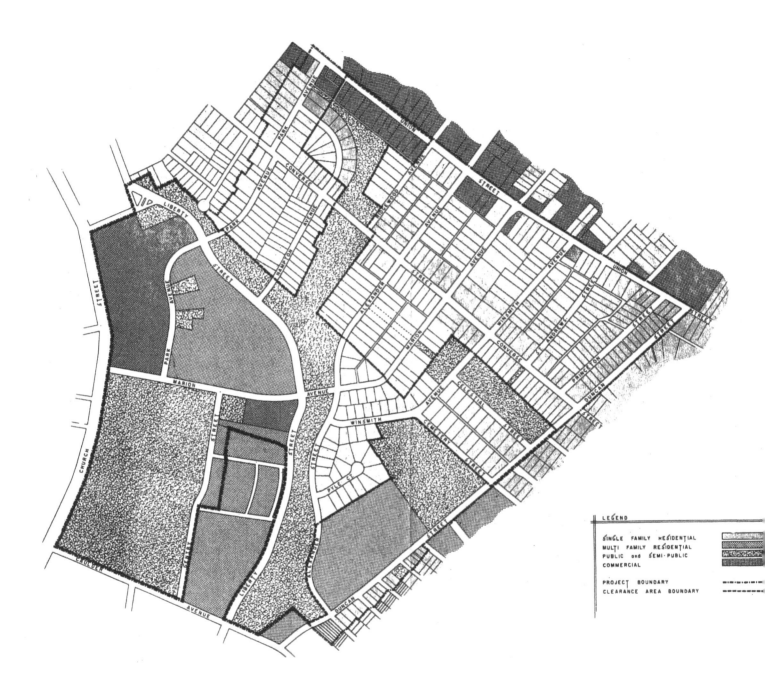

This city map shows the affected areas where homes and businesses were cleared on the Southside.

LEGEND

SINGLE FAMILY RESIDENTIAL
MULTI FAMILY RESIDENTIAL
PUBLIC and SEMI-PUBLIC
COMMERCIAL

PROJECT BOUNDARY   —·—·—·—·—
CLEARANCE AREA BOUNDARY   —————————

Urban Renewal and Model Cities in Depth

~Nancy Moore~

—Urban Renewal—

Under the 1949 federal housing law, urban renewal provided funds to clear areas dominated by substandard housing for the purpose of providing decent, safe, and sanitary housing. If a house could be repaired for less than 50 percent of the worth of the property, it was called "substandard." A "dilapidated" house cost more than 50 percent of its worth to repair and became a candidate for razing.

There were many substandard and dilapidated houses in the Cemetery Street area in the late 1960s. Because of the presence of so many "shotgun houses," such sections of the city suffered three times the density of housing of largely white areas.

The condition of a house or business was decided by awarding points upon the inspection of each house. A building could fall into four categories: standard, rehab-able, structurally substandard and requiring clearance, and clearance warranted by blighting influences. A total of 1,000 points covered 26 areas, ranging from the foundation to plumbing fixtures.

A sound building might be condemned not only for failing to rack up the required number of points, but also to make way for redirected or improved streets, as was the case with South Liberty Street. A more slippery category was clearance because of "blighting influences," such as excessive density of dwellings, inadequate street layout, or "incompatible uses or land use relationship," usually the mixing of residential, commercial, and manufacturing. Each city applying for Urban Renewal grants had a master plan that determined the highest and best use of land. In effect, whole areas might be razed and rezoned under "blighting influences." In Spartanburg's Cemetery Street project, only 37 homes—or less than 4 percent of the residential buildings—were condemned for blight. The rest came down for "blighting influences."

Determining whether a building should be rehabilitated was complex. About 20 percent of the 985 buildings in the Cemetery Street Project were scheduled for rehabilitation, provided that the owner was willing to undertake it. An initial appraisal evaluated the worth of a building; it was followed by another appraisal to evaluate the worth after repairs. Repairs had to begin 30 days after the city mailed a letter, which detailed both required and suggested improvements. Two inspections followed repairs, one immediately after repairs and one 60 days later. The average rehabilitation grant was $3,500, with about a third of the owners qualifying.

Like homeowners and renters, businesses received information about moving options and had to sign that they had read the information. The city promised to help with the relocation of Cemetery Street businesses during an expected relocation period of three years. Relocation payments, moving expenses, and property losses could be compensated for by as much as $25,000 for each business. The total amount set aside for moving and relocation expenses for businesses on the Southside was $425,225 or an average of about $5,500 per affected business.

The Cemetery Street project cost $8.7 million, an amount equal to an expense of $37 million in June 2004 dollars. That included the purchase of 493 parcels at $4.7 million and costs for surveying, planning, legal services, appraising, demolition, and moving and relocation. Spartanburg picked up the tab for slightly over $1 million of that total, most of it as in-kind services, such as site preparation valued at $413,000. The remaining funds for the local match came from the Model Cities program. Through grant writing, the

In the 18 years from 1959 to 1977, the city spent at least $17 million dollars on four Urban Renewal projects:
- Gas Bottom or R-1
- Highland or R-4
- Cemetery Street or R-14
- Southside I or R-20.

In these projects, it demolished about 1,200 houses, rehabilitated approximately 400, and relocated nearly 900 families and 310 individuals.

city invested one local dollar of in-kind services for each $21 in federal funds. City employees carried out demolition activities, though appraisals and legal expenses were contracted to private firms.

Where did the displaced families and individuals go? As was usually the case with Urban Renewal all over the United States, many settled within walking distance of their old houses, mainly in the Duncan Park area and in the Crescent Avenue area. The dispersal under urban renewal became the first big push for housing integration in Spartanburg.

In the end, the final economics of urban renewal stirred polemic differences across the United States, with most social scientists eventually condemning the effort. In the case of the Cemetery Street Project, the city would re-plat the acquired 493 parcels into about 160 parcels and estimated their worth to be only $1.3 million when purchased for redevelopment. (The land was discounted to encourage buyers for redevelopment under strict zoning.) The condemned parcels had originally been appraised as worth $4.7 million, a "loss" of $3.4 million. Only a small part of the loss was in such changes as eight parcels newly devoted to parks and playgrounds.

— MODEL CITIES —

Model Cities paid for projects alongside of urban renewal. For example, it cleaned and fenced the overgrown and abandoned cemetery for which the Cemetery Street Project was named. However much the two programs may have been confused, the concept and focus of the Model Cities program differed from that of urban renewal. Model Cities was implemented by the new Housing and Urban Development Department (HUD) in 1966, in part to correct the limitations and abuses of urban renewal. It was a social and economic arm designed to build neighborhoods, not just housing. It sought to increase health, education, and jobs and to reduce crime. In pursuit of these goals, Model Cities brought more than $7 million dollars into the city from 1969 to 1974 and provided the leverage for funneling in even more dollars.

According to the grant application for the first year, Model Cities built its citizen participation on the base of the African-American community's existing 49 social and sympathy clubs in the four Model Cities areas. The "Sympathy Clubs," as their name implied, were to show compassion to people in need. Among the Sympathy and Social Clubs in the Cemetery Street area were the Baptist Side Sympathy Club, the Phyllis Goins Sympathy Club, the Jolly Sixteens, the Silver Lockets, the Moon Glowers, The La Faus-Phyllis Goins, the One Nighters, the Jolly Eights, Entre Nous, and the Exotics-Tobe Hartwell.

During the planning phase in Spartanburg, the Model Cities staff conducted many meetings with neighborhood residents to determine needs. In the minutes of the meeting of the Model Neighborhood Authority from July 3, 1969, Dewey Tullis, Model Cities executive director, reported that "there had been 20 study group meetings with approximately 650 in attendance; and 17 general meetings with approximate attendance of 500." By the time of the first year of funding in 1970, the grant application claimed that there had been a survey of 10 percent of the area and 420 meetings, involving approximately 15,200 people of the total of 40,000 in the Model Cities areas. Eighteen meetings took place just in May 1970. People were being consulted and informed.

Each of the four Model Cities areas elected a representative to a Model Neighborhood Authority, which also had appointed members. The first winners and the number of votes cast were reported to City Council on June 5, 1970: Roselle Thompson, 23 votes; Robert Davis, 11; L.L Turner, 43; R. L. Graham, 72. The appointed members of the Neighborhood Authority included some of the best-known names of the African-American community, including: Cammie Clagett and the Reverends B.T. Sears and C.M. Johnson. So many members of the Neighborhood Authority were ministers that they had to change meeting times in the period of concentrated summer revivals. Mayor Robert Stoddard also counts Dr. J.C. Bull, a physician and brother to Clagett, and the Reverend Leon Pridgeon as supporters.

Chaired by Mayor Stoddard, the Spartanburg Model Neighborhood Authority met monthly, often for two- or three-hour sessions of information, questions, and reports on the problems—for example, the need for additional lighting in specific areas. Model Cities, though funded for only three years, still survives in the Spartanburg social order. Through the use of Model Cities funding in whole or in part, Spartanburg began a pre-trial sentencing program, the Boys Home, and the Girls Home. It helped build or initially staff both the C.C. Woodson and the T.K. Gregg Recreation Centers. Model Cities ran the first large-scale comprehensive daycare programs to help mothers of young children get an education or go to work, escaping welfare. Spartanburg Methodist College trained early childhood teachers and teachers' aides with Model Cities scholarships; for many students it was their first opportunity to attend college. Likewise, USC Upstate received scholarships for students from the Model Cities area, providing the initial critical mass for integration.

Model Cities also changed the face of city staff. Through programs for training police and fire cadets, Model Cities initiated the hiring of African-Americans in the city's Public Safety Department. Model Cities also boosted the Community Relations program. Dewey Tullis recalls that when he was hired as the program's assistant, the paint wasn't dry covering up the "colored" and "white" signs over separate bathrooms in City Hall.

✧ Dr. Nancy Moore is a retired English professor and former dean of arts & sciences from the University of South Carolina Upstate. In 2002 she taught a senior seminar at USC Upstate on urban renewal and its impact nationally and locally.

✧ Biographies

Raymond Floyd, photographer for *South of Main*, was born in Orangeburg and graduated from Claflin College. He moved to Spartanburg in 1963 when he was hired as the first-ever African-American art teacher in District Seven. He taught drawing, painting, sculpture and crafts for 30 years at Carver Junior High, before retiring in 1993. He has been a professional photographer since that time, having taken photography classes through the Greenville Museum of Art. He shares a photography studio with two other local photographers and shoots several weddings a year.

Beatrice Hill, one of the compilers of this history, was born in Tobe Hartwell Apartments and has had a lifelong interest in the history of her neighborhood. She attended school at Carrier Street Elementary, Highland Elementary, and Mary H. Wright, and graduated from Carver High School. She worked at Spartanburg Regional, Hoechst Fibers and Michelin Tire before retiring to become a substitute elementary and middle school teacher in District 7. In 1979 she coordinated the first Tobe Hartwell neighborhood reunion, which drew 300 people to her backyard. In preparation for a subsequent neighborhood reunion in 1999, she put together a committee of eight people and worked on a booklet with pictures from the early years.

Born on South Liberty Street, **Brenda Lee**, another of the compilers of this history, has lived on the Southside her entire life. She is a 1966 graduate of Carver High School and attended the University of South Carolina. She was the 1998 recipient of the E. Lewis Miller Award for leadership in Spartanburg and has served on numerous local boards including the Spartanburg Development Council and the Wofford College President's Advisory Committee. She served as a member of the S.C. House of Representatives from 1995 to 2005 and currently is a member of the regulatory staff and outreach manager of the S.C. Lifeline and Link-up Programs. Brenda also collects books by African-American woman authors.

The Hub City Writers Project is a non-profit organization whose mission is to foster a sense of community through the literary arts. We do this by publishing books from and about our community; encouraging, mentoring, and advancing the careers of local writers; and seeking to make Spartanburg a center for the literary arts.

Our metaphor of organization purposely looks backward to the nineteenth century when Spartanburg was known as the "hub city," a place where railroads converged and departed.

At the beginning of the twenty-first century, Spartanburg has become a literary hub of South Carolina with an active and nationally celebrated core group of poets, fiction writers, and essayists. We celebrate these writers—and the ones not yet discovered—as one of our community's greatest assets. William R. Ferris, former director of the Center for the Study of Southern Cultures, says of the emerging South, "Our culture is our greatest resource. We can shape an economic base … And it won't be an investment that will disappear."